My Aymond Family

From

Avoyelles

Martha Aymond Bordelon

and

Ordean Gaspard Aymond

Table of Contents

To my mother,

Ordean Gaspard Aymond

My mother, Ordean Gaspard Aymond, had a burning desire to uncover the forefathers of her family as well as the family of her husband. It began in 1979 when she attended a final class on Louisiana History with me at Louisiana State University. My instructor was Dr. Sue Eakin who was extremely knowledgeable and made the class so interesting that you looked forward to the next meeting. During this final class, Dr. Eakin spoke about the history of Avoyelles Parish. My mother's interest in her own ancestors was so aroused by Dr. Eakin that she and my father, Carol J. Aymond, Sr. spent the next 20 years traveling to different areas of the state and throughout the United States searching for answers. Her goal was to publish a book with her findings. You will see what she intended to be the introduction to this "book" written in her own hand on the following page. She accumulated boxes of notes, legal documents, and books during her search. It is from these that I have tried to organize and finish what she began so many years ago. I hope that this effort would have met or exceeded her expectations. So, Mom, this is for you.

Martha Aymond Bordelon

This was to be the introduction of the book, which my mother, Ordean Gaspard Aymond, planned to write on the Aymond family. This was her draft copy, written in her handwriting.

Marie-Odile PÉRÈS
GÉNÉALOGISTE
24, Quai Rouget de Lisle
67000 STRASBOURG
Tél. (88) 35.62.85

Mrs. Carol J. AYMOND
RFD I BOX 280

COTTONPORT, LA 71321

U.S.A.

Strasbourg, 22d April 1983

Dear Mrs. AYMOND,

Since you wrote to me and sent credit I have been trying on the
AYMOND family in different places of Bas-Rhin which I though could
be the right localities, sounding nearly like "Mortsi..., bishop
district of Strasbourg" ; beeing :
- MERTZWILLER (Mortsweiler)
- MORSCHWILLER (Mortzweiler)

So I checked both parish records for catholics for marriages around
1740 to 1770 and baptisms for about 1730-1755 in order to find some
AYMON-AYMOND or other spellings entries.

This failed completely in both places.
Now, it would be very important to have a copy of the record for
which you sent certificate (marriage 1771 at Baton Rouge, St James
church) for I think I could see exactly how this name is like and
guess the exact place from this document.

The bishops district of STRASBOURG (not Starusbour of course) was
large enough to have many places searched and namely :

- Morschwiller in Upper-Rhine in fact : Niedermorschwiller nowadays
- Merzig (near Sarreguemines) but not very likely as this place could
  be bishop district of METZ
- St MORITZ perhaps nowadays (St Maurice near Villé)

Time is so very quickly spent that your credit is already at an
end ; the next time I have an opportunity to be in COLMAR, I will
check for Niedermorschwiller, in the Haut-Rhin archives, and the
same for Saint Maurice ; but I cannot do any extra research for
you in both places now, as I already spent all time with research
in the other two places.

Sorry I could not do better for the moment ; when the place is not
well known, it is sometimes very difficult to find this first, then
of course everything seems easy.

                                    Very sincerely.

Chapter 1: The History of Alsace, France in the 1700's

Why did our ancestors move to Louisiana from Alsace, France in the 1700's?

Where did the Aymond family originate. Why did they come to Louisiana? These answers may be found with our earliest ancestor in Louisiana, Michael Aymond and his wife Catherine Aron Aymond.

I've asked myself why our ancestors would travel across the ocean to move to a land about which they knew so little. I've tried to concentrate my efforts in researching Alsace on the years preceding the immigration of Michael and Catherine Aron Aymond who left France during the 1740's or 50's. My question was, "What was happening in that area of France at that time to make them want to leave?" After reading about France and Germany during the 1600's and 1700's, I did uncover a great deal of information about this area of the world that helped to explain their decision to leave France. According to history, France was in a constant state of war. The possession of the territory of Alsace in particular was a source of conflict between France and Germany for over 150 years. Due to these wars, there was much hardship in France, especially for the people of Alsace-Lorraine.

The Territory of Alsace-Lorraine

Alsace is one of the 26 regions of France. Alsace and Lorraine straddle the French and German borders. For about 150 years, the jurisdiction of the area of Alsace and Lorraine went back and forth between France and Germany many times:

In 817 and 843, after the partitioned empire of Charlemagne was organized, Alsace became part of Lotharingia. Alsace became part of the German duchy of Alemannia in 925, and remained German for 800 years. Alsace was placed under the French sovereignty again in 1648, with the "Thirty Years War". After the Franco-Prussian War (1870-1871), Alsace and Lorraine were incorporated into the German Empire which was when the term Alsace-Lorraine was used for the first time. After World War I, in 1919, Alsace-Lorraine was returned to France by the terms of the Treaty of Versailles. Finally, during World War II, the territory was ceded to Germany, but France regained it after Germany's defeat in 1945.

In Alsace and in Lorraine, the French language is dominant. In Alsace, a German dialect called Alsatian, is spoken but its use is decreasing. This region would be a unique place to visit not only because our ancestors originated from this area, but also because its culture contains both French and German elements.

Alsace is in the northeast corner along the Rhine River. It's made of two provinces: Bas-Rhine in the north, and Haut-Rhine in the south. It is a 30-mile-wide piece of land bordered by the Vosges Mountains to the west, on the north by Germany, to the south by Switzerland. Alsace's largest city is Strasbourg. The name "Alsace" comes from the German "Ell-sass", which means, "Seated on the Ill", a

Alsace Province

0   25
MILES

Mannheim

GERMANY

Strasbourg

Rhine River

FRANCE

LORRAINE PROVINCE

Colmar

FRANCHE-COMTE PROVINCE

Basel

SWITZERLAND

JOHN BLANCHARD / *The Chronicle*

river in Alsace. It was made as one of the provinces of France in the 17th century under the kings Louis XIII and Louis XIV. France and Germany fought over the possession of Alsace for over 100 years. It changed hands four times between France and Germany between 1871 and 1918. The language of Alsace was a German language called Alsatian. Today, most of these people speak French, the language of the country they have been a part of for most of the past.

Coat of arms of the county of Alsatia.

Alsace, which is on the border of Germany, was more closely tied to Germany. In the 17th century, the French Empire began to expand and the German Empire began to fail, these border territories came to be under the rule of France. Although resistance and revolt to the French rule continued until 1766 at which time they became completely French-ruled. While Lorraine lost its German characteristics, and became a French-speaking area, Alsace, being further east and closer to Germany, maintained distinct Germanic culture, heritage, language, and identity. The lax French rule in this area of France led to the Alsatians remaining mostly Germanic instead of moving more towards French culture. Reunified Germany exploited this ethnic characteristic of Alsace to justify their claims on the region. While it is a matter of fact that France rules Alsace, much of their loyalty is to Germany. German nationalists point out that there are almost no Frenchmen who live in Alsace and, therefore, it should belong with Germany or Switzerland, or should be independent.

The 30 Years' War

The 30 Years' War, which was fought between 1618 and 1648, had life-changing effects on the people of Germany and Alsace. It destroyed more than 50% of the population in Alsace and many of the people from Switzerland, Germany, France, and other countries moved in. This war was fought for many reasons, one of them being a religious conflict between Protestants and Catholics in the Holy Roman Empire. France was Roman Catholic, but was also a rival of the Holy Roman Empire.

The area of Alsace was one of the major battlegrounds for this war, which was one of the most destructive wars in European history. It was mostly fought in what is now Germany, but at one time or another, involved most of the countries of Europe. The result of this war was major destruction of this entire region. It resulted in famine, disease, and bankruptcy of many of the powers. One thing that contributed to the destructive nature of this war was that the armies were expected to be self-funding from whatever they could take from the settlements where they attacked. This resulted in lawlessness that caused many hardships on the people living in that area. Many people in Germany, up to one-third, lost their lives during this war. Many Alsatians died and many others left the area.

In 1648, the Thirty Years' War was ended with the Peace of Westphalia. In this agreement, France annexed part of Alsace and some nearby territory.

1715: Louis XIV Dies

The death of Louis XIV in 1715 left France rich in glory but poor in wealth. In 1714, when John Law, a Scottish financier and adventurer, came to France, he renewed his friendship with the nephew of King Louis XIV, the Duke of Orleans. The duke, Philippe d'Orléans, became Regent of France after the king's death in 1715. The heir to the throne, Louis XV was only five years old at the time, so the regent served as ruler. John Law was an authority on banking and money circulation. The duke requested Laws advice and help in straightening out France's financial problems due to many years of overspending under Louis XIV.

1717: John Law (died in 1729) establishes the Louisiana Company to develop the Mississippi Valley for France

John Law suggested that he could liquidate the government's debt by a system of credit with paper money. In May, 1716, John Law set up the General Private Bank which developed the use of paper money. Much of the bank's capital was made up of government bills and notes. In August 1717, he bought the Mississippi Company to help the French colony in Louisiana. Law was the Chief Director of this company and was given authorization by France for a trade monopoly in the West Indies and North America. This bank was called the Royal Bank (Banque Royale) because the notes were guaranteed by the King of France. The bank began issuing more notes than it had coinage to back up. This led to economic inflation and a bank run when the new paper money lost half of its value. In 1720, the over issuing of bank notes led to the ruin and crumbling of the system. Law fled to Brussels in December of 1720, but his Company of the West was responsible for the development of Louisiana.

Law advertised the Mississippi land as one of plenty. In order to get the trade monopoly for Louisiana, John Law's company had to assure the colony's defenses and bring 6,000 colonists and 3,000 African slaves in 25 years. According to Glenn Conrad's book, The German Coast, John Law and his Company of the West recruited pioneers for settlement in the New World. Many of these people who settled the German Coast of Louisiana were from Alsace, the Rhineland, and Switzerland. The first wave of immigrants arrived in the early1700's and settled in St. Charles Parish. This area became known as the German Coast. The second wave arrived during the late 1740's and 50's and settled in St. John the Baptiste Parish. This area was referred to as the Second German Coast. It was during this time that I believe Michael and Catherine Aymond, with their two children, came to Louisiana.

1756: Seven Years War

The Seven Years' War (1756-63) was the last major conflict before the French Revolution. It involved all the great powers of Europe. France, Austria, Saxony, Sweden, and Russia were aligned on one side against Prussia, Hanover, and Great Britain on the other. The main points of the war between Great Britain and France involved overseas colonial struggles. Several of the war's battles were fought in North America, where it was called the French and Indian War.

Though the first few years of the war were successful for France, in 1759 things changed and they were defeated. France formed an alliance with Spain in 1761, but continued to be defeated throughout 1762. In 1763, they signed the Treaty of Paris, which confirmed the loss of French possessions in North America and Asia to the British. France also finished the war with very heavy debts, which they struggled to repay for the remainder of the 18th century.

1763: The Treaty of Paris

The Treaty of Paris was signed on February 10, 1763 by the kingdoms of Great Britain, France and Spain, with Portugal in agreement, it ended the Seven Years' War/French and Indian War. France lost control of Louisiana to the United Kingdom of Great Britain. All of Louisiana east of the Mississippi River, except the Isle of Orleans, went to Great Britain. Louisiana west of the Mississippi and the Isle of Orleans went to Spain.

Many military officials and others stayed behind in the colony. Lands were granted to these Frenchmen who remained behind. Therefore, many families of French origin came to live among the German-speaking farmers.

1789: Factors leading to the French Revolution

The French Revolution was a dangerous time to be alive in France...and Alsace was no exception. Many people were executed and many left for fear that they would be next. There were several factors that contributed to the beginning of the Revolution of 1789.

Near Bankruptcy of France

Many wars had been fought during the forty years preceding the Revolution. France had participated in most of most of these wars. These wars had a significant impact on the French treasury. Maintaining the French army and supporting allies during these wars depleted the French treasury.

France had two privileged orders, the nobility and the Catholic Church. Previously, the government was taxing only the common people and using this revenue to cover debts owed to aristocrats and other lenders. Louis XVI considered taxation of France's two privileged orders: the nobility and the Catholic Church. In 1787, the king's government convened a body of nobles and clergy called the Assembly of Notables as a consultative body. The nobles and clergy opposed the taxation of their orders and in May, the Assembly of Notables was dismissed. A larger consultative body, the Estates General, was convened. It consisted of members of the Church, called the First Estate; members of nobility, called the Second Estate; and all others, called the Third Estate. Plans were made for this body to meet in early 1789.

Loss of Work and Lack of Food

The high cost of food was another factor that contributed to the French Revolution. France's population in 1700 was 19 million. It grew to between 24 and 26 million without an increase in food production. The farmers consumed over 80 percent of what they grew, so if their harvest fell, many people went hungry. Storage of grain and government planning was insufficient in order to plan for these times of decreased production. In July 1788, farmers had their worst harvest when a hailstorm destroyed their crops. In addition to this, there was much unemployment. In Paris, the construction workers were without work. People lost their homes and had little to eat. The few people who were still employed spent most of their wages on buying bread to eat. As the bread became scarcer, its price rose. The Church, in an effort to help, handed out bread and milk. Getting little relief from their hunger, people began to riot. A program to import food and forbid the exporting of grain was implemented. This program had little success because of the frozen rivers and canals, which hampered transportation.

Extravagance of Royalty

The extravagance of royalty was another factor that led to the French Revolution. Lavish spending of the noble class, especially the court of Louis XVI and Marie Antoinette at Versailles continued despite the financial burden on the populace. Also, the ideas that King Louis XVI had absolute power due to divine right that he had been picked by God, was not readily believed as it had been in the last decades. The common people resented the monarch ruling with unlimited authority and power. The peasants and wage earners resented their privileges and dominance. The poor rural clergy resented the aristocratic bishops. The Protestants resented the Catholic control and influence on institutions of all kinds.

During the first days of the revolution, on June 1789, 576 out of 577 members from the Third Estate signed the Tennis Court Oath. The name was taken because of the meeting place, on an actual indoor tennis court. They began to call themselves the National Assembly, which was a legislature. They wanted the creation of a parliamentary system like the British. They took a solemn oath not to separate until the constitution of the kingdom was established. They pledged to continue to meet until a constitution had been written. This was a revolutionary act that showed that political authority would come from the people and their representatives and not from the monarch. The actions of the Third Estate forced Louis XVI to order the clergy and nobility to join with the Third Estate.

1789: The Storming of the Bastille

On July 14, 1789, in response the King's firing of Jacques Necker, his finance minister, the people in Paris marched in the streets. Demonstrators threw stones at the Cavalry who were trying to disperse them. The people called for the crowds to arm themselves, and they did. Soldiers also joined the crowds in looting and demonstrating. To obtain more guns and gunpowder, a crowd of about 80,000 people stormed the Bastille, an old fort in the city that housed about 7 prisoners. Several of the garrison soldiers were killed defending the Bastille, and 98 attackers were also killed.

The people in Paris saw this as a symbol of their authority and felt that they had taken control of the city. The king gave in and endorsed the new order in Paris. He appointed sympathizers of the people as municipal authorities, and armed people, called the National Guard, replaced his troops.

Outside of Paris, people were also rebelling. Where life was the hardest for peasants, they attacked more successful peasants as well as the grand manor houses and castles of nobles. They burned title deeds and searched for grain. Paying taxes to nobles was over. Many of the nobles who resisted were killed and their houses burned down.

1790: Abolition of Feudal Privileges

In 1790, better weather made better harvests that many took to mean that God was siding with the revolution. The National Assembly also moved to put all religion under its authority. They thought that the revolution conformed to Christian principles. They wanted the government to oversee the election of pastors, bishops, and clergymen to swear loyalty to this plan. Violence broke out between supports of the revolution and defenders of the Church. Louis XVI was not in favor of this, and the public cast more suspicion upon him.

On August 4, the National Assembly made the abolition of feudal privileges official. Nobles were no longer allowed to charge dues or hold exclusive hunting rights. They also removed nobles as makers of law and their courts were abolished. Nobles also were not exempt from paying taxes. The National Assembly also ended the obligation to pay tithes to the Church.

1791: Declaration of the Rights of Man and Citizen

In June 1791, Louis XVI wrote a note denouncing the revolution and fled with his family. He was caught on the border of the Austrian Netherlands and was returned to his palace. He was basically a prisoner and the National Assembly suspended his powers.

The National Assembly issued the Declaration of the Rights of Man and Citizen on August 27. This was a statement of principles to educated and encourages the love of liberty. It also included man's right to liberty, to resist oppression, and a right to property. It stated that all "men" were equal before law and that they should be presumed innocent until proven guilty by a court of law. It also stated that there should be freedom of religion.

The National Assembly had declared itself sovereign, but wanted the cooperation of the King. Louis stated that he agreed with the "spirit" of the constitution, but expressed concerns about specific points. Many viewed this as opposition. Animosity was spread against the king and many looked upon him with suspicion.

King Louis Accepts the New Constitution

On September 13, 1791, the King accepted the new constitution. There was much rejoicing and the revolution appeared to be complete. In the new constitution, protections were added for property owners stemming from fears that a complete democracy would lead to the redistribution and sharing of property. Also, the king would have limited veto powers, no control over the army, no authority over local governments, and he could send no representatives to serve in parliament. In addition, judges were to be elected and voting was to be by all who paid taxes. The constitution also guaranteed all men the freedom to speak, write, or print his opinions, provided he did not abuse this privilege. The taxes paid by a person would be based on the amount of their wealth.

Many of the royalty and nobles fled from France. With them also went the orders for lace, dresses, and other goods. Unemployment began to rise in these areas and international trade was down. For a second year, the harvests had failed. Hunger and hardship remained common for the people of France. It was said that the aristocrats were trying to prolong the hunger to bring the common people to their knees.

In October 1791, after a banquet at the royal palace, newspapers described it as an orgy that included insults to the revolution. Another mob of 7,000, made mostly of women, descended upon Versailles and the National Assembly. They invaded the royal apartments and killed bodyguards. They threatened to cut off Marie-Antoinette's head and fry her liver. She and her son fled through a secret passageway. After this, the king and queen, their children, and a few servants, went to live in the old Paris palace less splendid than Versailles.

The National Assembly outlawed any "unofficial demonstrations" under the penalty of death. The people in Paris still suspected that the deputies of the National Assembly were not sympathetic to their plight.

In the coming year, the following events took place: In November, the National Assembly nationalized the Church lands. In April, they issued paper money backed by the value of these lands.

1799: Napoleon Bonaparte Seizes Power

Napoleon returned to Paris from Egypt in August 1799, after hearing of the military crisis facing France. The moderates gave Napoleon the job of getting rid of the Consulate, which was accomplished when he seized control of France on November 9-10 in the Coup de Brumaire. Napoleon became Premier Consul of France, and imposed an authoritarian constitution on the country. During the winter of 1800 he reorganized the country, centralizing the economy, justice, education and the administration. He created a new army, using able-bodied Frenchmen rather than the upper-class and nobility. He began his bid for power, eventually controlling most of western Europe (except Britain and Portugal). He put into place a civil code and religious freedom. In 1804, in the presence of the Pope, he crowned himself emperor. His expansionism stopped in Russia, where a shortage of food and forage forced his troops' retreat in the midst of winter. A brief comeback after exile to Elba ended at Waterloo in 1815.

Spain returned its territory to France in 1800 through a secret deal in which the French, under Napoleon Bonaparte, promised to set up Spanish rule in Italy. In 1803, the United States, under Thomas Jefferson, purchased a territory from France in a deal known as The Louisiana Purchase.

Back to the Question: Why did our ancestors move to Louisiana from Alsace, France in the 1700's?

I think that I now understand why Michael and Catherine, with their two children, decided to travel across the ocean to a land where they had never before been. They would be leaving their home, which was ravaged by war, where they had been struggling to survive, and had endured many hardships due to the many conflicts in that area. They must have decided that the move could afford them many opportunities that they would not have if they remained in France. The Civil records tell us that many of them obtained land in Louisiana through grants from lands of the royal domain. With the promise of land, religious freedom, and the opportunity to give a better life to their children, it was probably not a difficult decision to make.

Today's Facts about Alsace

Language	Although German dialects were spoken in Alsace for most of its history, the dominant language in Alsace today is French.
Cuisine	Alsatian cuisine, strongly based on Germanic culinary traditions, is marked by the use of pork in various forms. Traditional dishes include baeckeoffe, flammekueche, choucroute, and fleischnacka. Alsace is an important wine-producing region. *Vins d'Alsace* (Alsatian wines) are mostly white and display a strong Germanic influence. Alsace is also the main beer-producing *région* of France, thanks primarily to breweries in and near Strasbourg. Schnapps is also traditionally made in Alsace, but it is in decline because home distillers are becoming less common and the consumption of traditional, strong,
Symbolism	The stork is a main feature of Alsace and was the subject of many legends told to children. The bird practically disappeared around 1970, but re-population efforts are continuing. They are mostly found on roofs of houses, churches and other public buildings in Alsace.
Topography	It is almost four times longer than it is wide, corresponding to a plain between the Rhine in the east and the Vosges mountains in the west
Economy	☐ hop harvesting (a small genus of flowering plants native to temperate regions of the Northern Hemisphere. The female flowers (often called "cones") are known as hops, and are used as a culinary flavoring and stabilizer, especially in the brewing of beer (half of French beer is produced in Alsace, especially in the vicinity of Strasbourg ☐ forestry development ☐ automobile industry ☐ tourism ☐ potassium chloride (until the late 20th century) and phosphate mining

Air Traffic	There are two international airports in Alsace: * The international airport of Strasbourg in Eztzheim; The international Euro Airport Basel-Mulhouse-Freiburg, which is the seventh largest French airport in terms of traffic Strasbourg is also two hours away from one of the largest European airports, Frankfurt Main.
Religion	Most of the Alsatian population is Roman Catholic, but largely because of the region's German heritage, a significant Protestant community also exists: today, the EPAL (a united Lutheran-Reformed church) is France's second largest Protestant church

Chapter 2: Michael and Catherine Aron Aymond

Michael and Catherine Aron Aymond were natives of Strasbourg, Alsace, France now the Department of Bas-Rhin, France. Both of their children, Marie and Jean, were born in Strasbourg, France as well. After immigrating to the United States, they resided in St. John the Baptist Parish, Louisiana. This had to have taken place before 1771, as their daughter Marie was married in St. James Parish during that year.

According to Glenn Conrad's book: <u>Saint Jean Des Baptiste Des Allemands</u>, the First German Coast, St. Charles Parish, was one of the earliest settled areas of Louisiana. These farmers contracted with John Law's Company to cultivate the wilderness of Louisiana. They came from regions of Germany, Bohemia, Switzerland, and Hungary. Most of them were natives of Alsace, the Palatinate and Baden. Many of their names were translated from German in to French names. Jacob became Jacques, Wilhelm became Guilaume, Zwaig means "twig" so he became Labranche. These farmers of St. Charles parish worked with their slaves in the fields. By the 1740's and 50's, they began showing signs of prosperity. Governor Kerleiec, who was governor of the French colony of Louisiana between 1753-1763, requested that the French government recruit more German colonist for Louisiana.

It was during this second wave of German immigration, in the late 1740's and early 1750's, that I believe our ancestors Michael and Catherine Aron Aymond came to Louisiana. The Germans that came before them already occupied the areas of St. Charles parish, the German Coast. Therefore, they moved on into the virgin lands of what would be the parish of St. John the Baptiste des Allemands and would be referred to as the Second German Coast.

Most of the German Coast settlers in Louisiana came from the Rhineland, the land on either side of the Rhine River; region of Germany, the German-speaking cantons of Switzerland, and other places today called, *Bayou des Allemands* and *Lac des Allemands* (meaning Germans' Bayou and Germans' Lake, in French). Many Germans came from the German-speaking region of Alsace-Lorraine in France, and some from Switzerland and Belgium. (Wikipedia) From the time of their arrival, the German immigrants began speaking French and intermarried with the early French settlers. Over the subsequent decades, they intermarried with the descendants of the latter as well as the Acadians. Together with other settlers, they helped create Cajun culture. For example: German settlers introduced the diatonic accordion to the region, which became the main instrument in Cajun music by 1900. (Wikipedia)

By the 1780 and 1790, families grew larger as children married and had their own families to support. Large farms were divided into smaller ones as children inherited their parents' property. Civil records show that in many instances, when the property was not sufficient to support the growing families, many would sell their small strips of land and move to another area where a larger parcel could be obtained. Therefore, many families that began on the German Coast were transplanted to areas such as Opelousas, Attakapas District, or the Lafourche country.

Marie Aymond

Marie was one of the two children that we know Michael and Catherine brought to Louisiana. She, like her brother Jean Pierre was born in Strasbourg, France. Unlike today, when a daughter was to be married, she had to obtain consent from her parents. On August 6, 1771, Marie obtained permission to marry Noel Etienne Arvieux, son of Pierre Arvieux and Marie Anderive of Este de Hute in Lower Languedoc. Languedoc is an area in the southern part of France. What follows is the original "Permission to Marry" and the English translation.

Husband: Michael Aymond
DOB: 1725 in Strasbourg, France
Married: About 1757 in Alsace, Strasbourg, France
Died: 1800
Buried: St. John the Baptist Parish

Wife: Catherine Aron
DOB: About 1725

Died: 1800
St. John the Baptist Parish, LA

Children:

Name	DOB - DOD	Married	Comments
Marie	Born in Strasbourg, France M: 8/6/1771 in St. James Parish	Noel Etienne Arvieux	Noel's parents were Pierre Arveux and Marie Anderive of "Estes de Hate in "Lower Languedoc", France.
Jean Pierre	Born about 1750 in Strasbourg, France M: 4/5/1785 in St. Louis Parish, New Orleans	Marianne Joffrion DOB: 3/22/1758 at Pointe Coupee	Marianne's parents were Pierre Joffrion and Marianne Valleau (Vallo)

Michael and Catherine were natives of Strasbourg, Alsace, now the Department of Bas-Rhin, France. Both of their children were born in Strasbourg, France as well. After immigrating to the United States, they resided in St. John the Baptist Parish. This had to have taken place before 1771, as their daughter Marie was married in St. James Parish at that time.

This is the Permission to Marry
given by Michael and Catherine
Aron Aymond for their daughter

This is the English translation of the
Permission to Marry given by
Michael and Catherine Aron Aymond
for their daughter Marie.

Translated by Ordean G. Aymond.

Year 1771 the 6th of August gave nuptial benediction after publication of 3

banns between Noel Etienne Arvieux son of Pierre Arvieux and Marie

Anderive of Este de Hute in Lower Languedoc and Marie Anne daughter of

Michel Aymond and Catherine Aron born at Mortze n (?) in Alsaca,

Bishorpic of Strasbourg both of St. Jean Baptiste parish. Made their marks

in presence of witnesses.

Jean Pomier   Pierre Keler

Guillaume Pivotaie

15

This Certificate of Marriage was obtained by Ordean G. Aymond. It shows that Marie and Noel Arvieux were married in St. James Church, located in St. James, Louisiana.

Certificate Of Marriage

Diocese Of Baton Rouge
Department Of The Archives
1800 S. Acadian Thruway P.O. Box 2028
Baton Rouge, La. 70821

This Is To Certify

That __Noel Etienne Arvieux, native of Este de Hate,__ __bishopric of the same name in Lower Languedoc,__

Son Of: __Pierre Arvieux & Marie Anderive__

and __Marie Aymon, born at Mortsi...(?), in Alsace,__ Bishopric of Starusbour,

Daughter Of: __Michel Aymon & Catherinne Aron__

were lawfully Married

on the __6__ Day of __August 1771__

According to the Rite of the Roman Catholic Church

in the presence of __Michel Schledr, Jean Pomier, Pierre Keler,__

and __Guillaume Pivoteau__ Witnesses.

A true and exact extract from the Marriage Register of

__St. James Church, St. James, La.__

Date __22 December 1982__ Vol. __1__ Page __15__ No. _____

Certified by _____
Archivist

Chapter 3: Jean Pierre Baptiste Aymond and Marianne Joffrion

Jean Aymond was born at Mortsi, Strasbourg, Alsace-Lorraine, France to Michael Aymond and Catherine Aron around 1750. This area is located on the border of France and Germany. As far as we know, his only sibling was Marie Aymond who was also born in Strasbourg, France. His parents immigrated to the United States and resided in St. John the Baptist Parish. This had to be before 1771, as their daughter Marie was married in St. James Parish at that time to Noel Etienne Arvieux.

Jean Pierre served in the military in January 1778, when he was 28 years old. His name appears on the U.S. Revolutionary War Rolls, 1775-1783. He was a Corporal in Hazen's Regiment. His Captain was Antoine Paulint.

Jean was the progenitor of the Aymond family here in Avoyelles. Jean (sometimes referred to as John) married Marianne Joffrion in St. Louis Parish, New Orleans, on April 5, 1785; he was 35 years old. The record states that two children, Pierre Aymond and Catherine Aymond, were therefore legitimized. Marianne was the daughter of Pierre Joffrion and Mariane Vallo, who were natives of La Rochelle, Renneu, France. Her father, Pierre, served in the Revolutionary War.

Jean and Marianne settled within the Post du Rapides in the mid 1780's. All seven of their children were listed as being born in Avoyelles Parish. Most of their children were married at Marianne's home after Jean had died in 1824.

In 1813, after being married for 28 years, Marianne filed suit against Jean (John) claiming that he was cruel and barbarous to her. The judge decreed a "separation from bed and board", awarded her one-half of John's property for support and maintenance, and directed her to live at the home of her son, Michael. Jean acknowledged that he and his wife could no longer live together in a peaceful manner and agreed to give her half of the property.

Three of their children, Peter, Michael, and Stephen moved to Avoyelles Parish when they each claimed 640 acres of property situated on Bayou do Lac, near the community of Hessmer.

The Revolutionary War

When the American Revolutionary War began, the colonials didn't have a real army. Each colony had as its own local defense, which consisted of its citizens. The Continental Army was created to coordinate the military efforts of the Thirteen Colonies against the rule of Great Britain. When tensions with Great Britain increased, they began to organize their militias in order to prepare for what they thought would be potential conflict. The Continental Army then consisted of all 13 colonies after 1776.

In order to join the army, soldiers had to be at least 16 years old or 15 with their parent's consent. Jean Pierre was 28 years old when he joined the military. He was a Corporal in Hazen's Regiment serving under Captain Antoine Paulint, I am convinced that this Jean Aymond is our ancestor, it has been debated because his birthdate is not shown on any of these war records. He is shown as a member of French descendants who settled in Avoyelles and fought in the American Revolution. He is listed as being in the New Orleans Militia; our Jean Aymond was married in New Orleans, showing that he was in that area. I have been unable to locate a record that "proves" this is the same Jean Aymond, I will continue to search for that elusive document.

⊰ancestry

Jean Aymond
in the U.S., Revolutionary War Rolls, 1775-1783

Name:	Jean Aymond
Gender:	Male
Military Date:	Jan 1778
Military Place:	USA
State or Army Served:	Continental Troops
Regiment:	Hazen's Regiment
Rank:	Corporal

Source Information

Ancestry.com. *U.S., Revolutionary War Rolls, 1775-1783* [database on-line]. Provo, UT, USA: Ancestry.com Operations, Inc., 2007.

Original data:

Revolutionary War Rolls, 1775-1783; (National Archives Microfilm Publication M246, 138 rolls); War Department Collection of Revolutionary War Records, Record Group 93; National Archives, Washington. D.C.

Description

This database is a collection of records kept by the U.S. National Archives listing men who fought for the colonies during the war. Each record provides the soldier's name, category, rank information, and NARA microfilm roll number to aid the researcher in locating the original record. Images of the records are also included. Learn more...

Husband: Jean Pierre Baptiste Aymond   Wife: Marianne Joffrion

DOB: About 1750 in Strasbourg,   DOB: March 23, 1758 Pointe Coupee
    Alsace, Lorraine, France   Died: January 1824 in Avoyelles Parish
Died: March 19, 1824   Parents: Pierre (1715) and
Avoyelles Parish   Marianne Vallo Joffrion
                  natives of La Rochelle, Rennes, France

  Buried: St. Paul Apostle Cemetery
    Avoyelles Parish
Married: April 5, 1785 St. Louis Parish, New Orleans
Parents: Michael (1725) & Catherine Aron Aymond

Name	DOB -Married - DOD	Married	Notes
Catherine (Marie)	DOB: before 4/5/1785	John Reed	John's parents were Charles Reed and Isabelle Aloron
Pierre (Peter)	DOB: before 4/5/1785 M: 1/19/1824 M: 1/2/1846	Eloise (Louise) Dauzat Melina Ducote	Eloise was the widow of Claude Recouly and daughter of Antoine Dauzat and Angelique Deshautell.
Jean Pierre II .	DOB: 1788 M: 4/3/1811 in Avoyelles DOD: 1833	Roseline Dauzat B: D: Before 2/1837	Book A, Page 35 Jean lived on Bayou Boeuf in Avoyelles Parish
Helen (Elena or Meline or Ellen)	DOB: 3/22/1790 Avoyelles M: c1804-05 DOD: 1862	Charles Fouquier (Fuqua) from Le Havre, France	
Michael	DOB: 3/7/1792 in Avoyelles Bapt. 11/20/1796 M: 5/7/1816	Theoline Dupuis Azelie Dupuis	Book A, page 149 Theoline was the daughter of Andre Dupuis and Justine Normand.
Severine	DOB: 1795 in Avoyelles M:	Rosalie Robert	

Etienne 'Stephen' Aymond	DOB. 9/27/1797 in Plaucheville
	M: 4/10/1815
	DOD. before 3/1866
		1.Sophie Lemoine
		   DOB: 8/17/1794
		   DOD: 7/6/1828
		2. Perrine Juneau
			Sophie was the daughter of Guillaume Lemoine and Marie Couvillion) Succession of Etienne: Book A, Page 101-102, 4/10/1815

Notes: Succession: Marksville Courthouse, Book A, Pages 101-102, 4/10/1815
    This Aymond family was the first of that name in Avoyelles per W. Nelson & L. Gremillion in
<u>Some Early Families of Avoyelles Parish, Louisiana.</u>

This document states: A Pay Roll of an Independent Company commanded by Captain Antoine Paulint in the Service of the United States of America and assigned to Colonel Moses Hazen Regiment for the month of January 1778. Shown as a Corporal in this regiment is Jean Aymond.

American Revolutionary War

Birth: unknown
Death: unknown

In this cemetery lie the unmarked graves of soldiers of French descent who settled in Avoyelles, having fought in the American Revolutionary War Battle of Baton Rouge under Galvez in 1779

Pointe Coupee Militia:
Major Antoine Bordelon
Jean Paul Decuir
Pierre Decuir
Charles Dufour
Joseph Gremillion
Joseph Joffrion
Augustin Juneau
Baptiste Lacour
Pierre Landreneau
Simon Lavallee
Jean B. Mayeux
Joseph Mayeux
Jean B. Olivier
Georges Olivo
Michel Pampolon
Jean Baptiste Rabalais
Riche'
Joseph Roy
Etienne St. Romain

With Gen. Lafayette:
Dominique Baldonide dit Coco, I

Attakapas Militia:
2nd Lt. Jacques Gaignard
Sgt. Louis Armand
Corp. Baptiste Guillory
Charles Jeansonne, fils
Noel Soileau

German Coast Militia:
Joseph Dubroc, II
Pierre Dupuis
Daniel Gaspard
Pierre Normand

Natchitoches Militia:
Brigadier Louis Armand

New Orleans Militia:
Jean Aymond
Etienne Plauche'

Mobile Militia:

Added by: CJ

Added by: CJ

 - CJK
Added: May. 30, 2012

21

> This document is a suit against Jean Aymond by his wife, Marianne Joffrion Aymond

To the Honorable K. M. Crumnier, Judge of the Parish of Avoyelles.

The petition Mary Ann Amon most respectfully represents that John Amon her husband has treated her for a long time past, and still continues to treat her in a manner so cruel, barbarous and altogether unbecoming a husband so undeserved by your petitioner that it is absolutely impossible for her longer to live with him as his wife. Your petitioner states that she shall be able to prove to the satisfaction of your honor acts of cruelty and barbarity such as has been represented and as or before stated, renders her unable longer to reside with the said John Amon as his wife. She further states that the said Amon's conduct has been such as to compel her your petitioner to quit his said John Amon's house, that he the said John refuses to allow her anything for her maintenance in consequence whereof she is reduced to the greatest imaginable disturbance. She therefore prays your Honor to cite the said John Amon to be and appear before your Honor to answer this complaint and that your Honor will decree between your petitioner and the said John Amon a perpetual separation from bed and board and further that your Honor will adjudge to your petitioner one half the said John Amon's property for her support and maintenance as is by the law in such cases directed and your petitioner as in duty bound will ever pray.

Enoch….. Louie

Counsel for Petitioner

Let a summons _____ and due notification be given to the defendant.

*K. Mcrummin

To the Hon.ble R. McCrimmin Judge of the Marine
of Argylles.

The Petition Mary Ann Amon most respectfully
represents, that John Amon her husband has treated
her for a long time past, and still continues to
treat her in a manner so cruel, barbarous and
altogether unbecoming a husband so undeserved
by your petitioner, that it is absolutely impossible for her longer to live with him as his
wife. Your Petitioner states that she shall be
able to prove to the satisfaction of your
Honor acts of cruelty and barbarity such as have
been represented, and as, as beforestated, render
her unable longer to reside with the said
John Amon as his wife. She further states
that his the said Amon's conduct has been
such as to compel her your Petitioner to
quit his the said John Amon's house, that
he the said John refuses to allow her anything for her maintenance & in consequence
whereof she is reduced to the greatest imaginable
distress. She therefore prays your Honor
to cite the said John Amon to be an ppear
before your Honor to answer this complaint
& that your Honor will decern between

perpetual separation from bed and board
and further that your Honor will adjudge
to your petitioner one half the said John
Amon's property for her use & and maintenance
as is by the law in such cases directed
And your petitioner as in duty bound will
ever pray &c

Enoch McLaine
Counsel for Petitioner

Let a summons issue and due notification be given to
the defendant — R. McCrimmin Judge

No. 155

Mary Ann Amon

  vs

John Amon

Filed March 15, 1813

Parish Court of the parish of Avoyelles, April 7, 1813

The parties' appearance in their own proper persons. The defendant acknowledges judgment that is to say he acknowledges that it is utterly impossible for himself and his wife to live together in a peaceable manner such as the laws direct and therefore agrees to give her half of the property which he now holds of which a legal Bill of Sale is passed this day to the plaintiff the plaintiff acknowledging himself perfectly satisfied with the division made and   in said Article of Sale as her part and portion of said estate. It is therefore ordered by the Court after due deliberation that a separation from bed and board take place between John Amon and his wife Mary Ann Amon .

  You are hereby directed to make Michael Amon's house your place of residence until the suit commenced by yourself against John Amon your Husband is finalized.

              Avoyelles, March 15th 1813

              K. Mcrummin

(Note: Michael Amon is the son of MaryAnn (Marianne) and John (Jean) Amon.)

Marianne vs Jean (John) Aymond

March 15, 1813

Mary Ann Amon
vs
John Amon

Filed march 15 1813

Witnesses present
James & _____
James le Clayton
mark
Micheal X Amon
his

Signed by the parties for
want of room below
John Amon père
Mary X ann Amon

Parish Court of the parish
of Avoyelles April 7 1813

The parties appeared in their own proper
persons. The defendant acknowledges Judgment that is to say he acknowledges that
it is utterly impossable for himself and his
wife to live together in a peaceble maner
such as the Laws direct and therefore
agrees to give her half of the property
which he now holds of which a legal Bill
of Sale is passed this day to the plaintiff
The plaintiff acknowledging herself perfectly
satisfied with the division made and expres
in said Articles of Sale as her part and portion
of said Estate. It is therefore ordered by the
Court after due deliberation that a sepperation afrom
bed and board take place between John Amon père
and his Wife Mary Ann Amon.

proper Mary ann Amon
You are hereby directed to make Micheal Amons
use your place of residence untill the Suit comm__
yourself against John Amon your Husband is fina__
divided. Avoyelles March 15th 1813
H. McCrimmon Gra__

Claim of 640 acres of property in
Avoyelles by Michael Amon, son of
Jean and Marianne Joffrion

December 25, 1813

No 1119 In pursuance of an act of Congress ___ the 27 February 1813 entitled an act giving further time for Registering Claim to Land in the Eastern & Western District of the Territory of Orleans now State of Louisiana.

Michael Amon claim Tract of Six hundred and forty acres of Land situated on Bayou do Lac in the Parish of Avoyelles, bounded on the lower side by Land of Charles Touchet and above by Land claimed by Peter Amon which Tract of Land has been occupied as required by Law.

Opelousas 25th Dec. 1813

26

Nº 1119 In pursuance of an act of April of thirty
the 27 February 1813 entitled un act giving
time for Registering Claim to Land in the Eastern &
Western District of the Territory of Orlean and
State of Louisiana

Michael Amon claim a Tract of
Six hundred and forty acres of Land situated
on Bayou du Lac Rou on the Parish of
Avoyelles. Bounded on the lower side by
Land of Charles Touchet, white and above
by Land claimed by Peter Amon — which
Tract of Land has been occupied as required
by Law.

Opelousas 26th Dec. 1813

Evidently Peter, Michel, & Stephen AMON
ARE Definitely brotherS!   SONS of Jean Amon (Aymond)
                            & MARIANE Joffrion

State of Louisiana

Parish of Avoyelles   No. 469

Sale of Land

Jean Amond, Jr.

    To

Jean Amond, Pere

Jean Amond, Jr. sells property to his father, Jean Amond, Pere

August 14, 1815

Today, the fourteenth day of the month of August, year of Grace, eighteen hundred and fifteen and of the Independence of the United States of America, the 40th and before me, Alexander Plauche', Judge of Avoyelles Parish, judge of the Court, authorized by law to function as Notary Public, performed in presence of witnesses, signed Mr. Jean Amond, fils of this parish who declares having sold, ceded and gives claim, transported now and forever to Mr. Jean Amond, pere, his inheritance in the parish of Avoyelles bordered on North cote by Samuel Glass, and South cote by Michel Amond and Jean Amond (the vendor) and east by Joseph Hooter for the sum of 500 dollars and the said Jean Amond Jr. declares he received and quart… the said land is without mortgages and Mr. Jean Amond, pere, signs by his ordinary mark of a cross and Judge and witnesses on same day, is certified.

Accepted by Jean Amond   X

Jean Amond

Marc Eliche

August 14th 1815

Alexander Plauche'

Judge of the Parish of Avoyelles

Jean Amond, Jr. sells property to his
father, Jean Amond, Pere

August 14, 1815

29

 ancestry

1830 United States Federal Census

Name:	**Jean Aymond**
Home in 1830 (City, County, State):	Avoyelles, Louisiana
Free White Persons - Males - Under 5:	2
Free White Persons - Males - 5 thru 9:	1
Free White Persons - Males - 10 thru 14:	1
Free White Persons - Males - 40 thru 49:	1
Free White Persons - Females - Under 5:	1
Free White Persons - Females - 10 thru 14:	1
Free White Persons - Females - 15 thru 19:	2
Free White Persons - Females - 30 thru 39:	1
Slaves - Males - 24 thru 35:	1
Free White Persons - Under 20:	8
Free White Persons - 20 thru 49:	2
Total Free White Persons:	10
Total Slaves:	1
Total - All Persons (Free White, Slaves, Free	11

Marriage License for Pierre (Jean &
Marianne) and Melina Ducote

January 2, 1846

Jean Pierre Aymond died on March 19, 1824 in Avoyelles Parish at the age of 74. He is in an unmarked grave for soldiers of French descent who fought in the American Revolutionary War, Battle of Baton Rouge with Galvez in 1779. The plaque which bears his name is located at St. Paul the Apostle Cemetery in Mansura, La.

Chapter 4: Etienne (Stephen) Aymond and Sophie Lemoine

Etienne was the seventh and youngest child of Jean Aymond and Marianne Joffrion. He was born on September 27, 1797 in Avoyelles Parish. He had four older brothers and two sisters. Etienne's baptism records were found under the Spanish writing of his name, Estevan Homo. His godparents were Jacob Hooter and Margaret Simon.

Etienne and his brothers and sisters seem to have grown up in somewhat of a tumultuous household. In 1813, when Etienne was 16 years old, after 28 years of marriage, his parents, Jean and Marianne separated. She claimed, according to the suit that: "he (Jean) treated her for a long time past, and still continues to treat her in a manner so cruel, barbarous and altogether unbecoming a husband so undeserved by your petitioner that it is absolutely impossible for her to live with him as his wife." The judge ordered that she move in with her son, Michael, who was just five years older than Etienne. He also awarded her one-half of her husband's property for her support and maintenance.

Etienne, along with his two brothers, Michel and Pierre, served in the 17th, 18th, and 19th Consolidated Regiment of the Louisiana Militia at the Battle of New Orleans during the War of 1812. According Randy Decuire, in his book entitled Avoyelleans at The Battle of New Orleans and the War of 1812, these three regiments represented Avoyelles, Rapides, Natchitoches, Catahoula, and Ouachita parishes in 1814 and 1815. He also stated that:

> "While several Avoyelles men received land grants for their service, many were denied pensions from Washington D.C. because the war department said their service was "not official because it happened after the treaty of peace was negotiated". (pp 6-7)

Although their service was after the treaty was negotiated, these men were sent to New Orleans to ensure that the English had left the area. After they arrived, they saw that the English had indeed vacated the area.

In February 1813, at sixteen years of age, Etienne (Stephen) claimed 640 acres of property in what previously was the Territory of Orleans at Bayou do Lac in Avoyelles Parish. In December, 1813, his brother Michael also claimed 640 acres of property in the same area. Both Michael's property and Stephen's property were both bounded by their older brother, Peter (Pierre) Amon. I can only believe that it was a relief for Stephen to be away from his parents' arguments.

Two years later, when Stephen was eighteen years old, he married Sophie Lemoine, daughter of Guillaume Lemoine and Marie Couvillion. Sophie was twenty-one years old. Stephen and Sophie married in a civil ceremony on April 10, 1815 at Mt. Carmel, Hydropolis in Avoyelles Parish, which was solemnized by a Catholic ceremony on March 19, 1824. They settled in Cocoville. After 15 years they moved to Dora Bend between Cottonport and Evergreen. They were plantation owners at Bayou Rouge in Avoyelles Parish.

After they had been married for thirteen years, she died on July 6, 1828 at the age of 34. Her last daughter, Sophie, was born in that year which leads me to believe that her mother died at that same time. This would also explain why the daughter was given her mother's name of "Sophie". Etienne and Sophie had a total of seven children.

One year later, Stephen married Perrine Juneau on August 25, 1829. From this marriage, he had twelve more children. The children included two sets of twins: Prudence and Prudent (1841), and Aulin and Auline (1844)

Stephen and Perrine Juneau Aymond appear on the Louisiana Census Records of 1840, 1850 and 1860. On the 1860 Census, it shows they are living at home with three children: Prudence, Auline, and Aulin. Stephen must have been considered relatively wealthy for the time because he owned property valued at $15,000, and personal property valued at $4,000 (Avoyelles Parish, P O Marksville, Roll 407 Book 1, page 360, dated August 30, 1860). This information was posted on "Ancestry" by Geneva Swis on November 14, 2007.

Etienne 'Stephen' Aymond died during the last part of 1860 or the very beginning of 1861 in Bayou Jacques, located in Avoyelles Parish at the age of 64. This is evidenced by the succession recorded in Louisiana Wills and Probate Records, 1756-1984 on January 13, 1862. Perrine Juneau Aymond and Joseph Aymond, his son, take an oath of "natural tutor" for the minor children of Etienne and Perrine, Germaine, Prudence, Oline, and Olin Aymond. He is buried in St. Paul's Cemetery in Mansura, LA.

Husband: Etienne 'Stephen' Aymond
DOB: September 27, 1797, Bayou Rouge
              Avoyelles Parish, LA
DOD: November 27, 1861, Bayou Jacques, Avoyelles
Married: April 10, 1815 in Mt. Carmel, Hydropolis
Christened: May 12, 1802, Bayou Rouge, Avoyelles, LA
Second Marriage: Perrine Juneau 1840
Parents: Jean Pierre Aymond (1750-1824)
          Marianne Joffrion (1758-1828)

Wife: Sophie Lemoine
DOB: August 17, 1794

DOD: July 6, 1828
Mother: Marie Couvillion
Father: Guillaume Lemoine

Children of Etienne and Sophie

Names	DOB - DOD	Married	Comments
Etienne Aymond II	DOB. 12/1815 M.: 12/5/1844 DOD: 1870 ?	Elodie Chenevert DOB: c1824	He was baptized on 12/7/1817 in Avoyelles Succession: Book H, Sept. 1870
Jean Baptiste Aymond	DOB: 3/9/1818 M: 12/6/1836	Mary Day	Book B1 Baptized on July 13, 1818 in Avoyelles
(Jean) Pierre Aymond	DOB: 1/1/1820 DOD: 5/19/1866	Celine/Selina Broussard DOB: c1821	He served in Civil War; buried in French Cemetery in Effie, LA. Succession: Book B, Page 154 Baptized: 6/11/1820 in Avoyelles
Guillaume / William Aymond	DOB: 1/27/1824 M: 7/4/1848 D. before 1870	Clarice Ducote DOB: c1832	Succession: Large Probate Book D, Pages 190-191, 8/12/1865
Elise/Eliza Aymond	DOB: 2/24/1822 M: 4/1/1839 M: 6/4/1866 D. before 2/1848	Cyprien Bonnette Charles Mason	She died of Yellow Fever Marriage to Charles Mason: Book B, Page 297 Family Meeting: Book A, Page 45 Baptized: 11/20/1822 in Avoyelles
Caroline Aymond	DOB: 4/28/1826M: 10/13/1840	Zenon Areaux DOB: c1815	Marriage in Stephen's home on Bayou Rouge: Book B2, p. 18 Succession: Book C, Page 268
Sophie Aymond	DOB: c182 M: 3/12/1846 M: 5/2/1854	Nichol Nicholson Paul Zenon "Degastile" Ducote	Book B2, p. 77 Marriage to Paul Ducote: Book B2, Page 356
Note: Book A, Marksville Courthouse St. Paul's Catholic Church, Mansura, Louisiana			

Children of Etienne Aymond and Perrine Juneau			
Adeline Aymond	DOB: M: 11/9/1847	Alexander Kimball	Marriage in home of Stephen on Bayou Jack: Book B2, Page 159
Joseph Aymond	DOB. c1834 M. 4/14/1858	Sarah Elvira Keller	Marriage in home of Stephen Aymond: Book B3, Page 43 Sarah was from St. Landry Parish
Valentine Aymond	DOB: c1836		
Emelia 'Melia' Aymond	DOB: c1838 M: 9/14/1854 M: 3/15/1866	Ovide Johnson Julien Juneau	Marriage to Julien Juneau: Book B or C, Page 283
Prudence Aymond	DOB. 1841 M. 12/16/1865	Hilaire Dauzat DOB: 1847	Prudence is buried in Moreauville Cemetery
Prudent Aymond	DOB. c1841 M. 6/19/1860	Celestine Marcotte DOB: 6/8/1858 DOD: 6/22/1934	Book B3, p. 122 Prudent Aymond: Durbe C.O's Co., La. Calvary
Gervais "Germaine" Aymond	DOB: c1842 M: 3/6/1862	Julie Mayeux DOB: 1844	Book B3, Page 180 Petition for a Family Meeting: Book E, Page 105
Aulin 'Olin' Aymond (Twin)	DOB: c1844 M: 7/11/1865	Julie Mayeux	He married the widow of his brother Book B3, Page 226
Auline 'Oline' Aymond (Twin)	DOB: c1844 M: 1/25/1866	Auguste Dauzat	
Zelia Aymond	DOB: 1850		
Clementine Aymond	DOB: M: 2/7/1846 M: 1/25/1862	William Turner Zenon Mayeux	Daughter of Perrine Juneau & Etienne Aymond, Bk. B2, p.75 Married William Turner at the home of Stephen Aymond, Book B2, Page 75 or 95
Isidore Aymond		Zena Armand m. on 4/13/1908	Daughter of Perrine & Etienne Book H, 750
Notes: Book A, Page 101-102, April 10, 1815, Property left to Sophie from her parents.			

Claim of 640 acres of property in Avoyelles by Stephen Amon, son
of Jean and Marianne Joffrion

February 27, 1813

No 1120 In pursuance of an act of Congress ___ the 27 February 1813 entitled an act giving further time for Registering Claim to Land in the Eastern & Western District of the Territory of Orleans now State of Louisiana.

Stephen Amon claims Tract of Six hundred and forty acres of land situated on Bayou do Lac in the Parish of Avoyelles, bounded below by land claimed by Peter Amon and above by Vacant Land which Tract of Land has been occupied as required by Law.

Opelousas 25th Dec. 1813

Stephen claims 640 acres of property in Avoyelles
Parish

No. 1120 In pursuance of an Act of Congress the 27 February 1813 entitled an act giving time for Registering Claims to Lands in the Eastern & Western Districts of the Territory of Orleans now State Louisiana

Stephen Amon claims a Tract of Six hundred and forty acres of Land situated on Bayou du Lac in the Parish of Avoyelles, Bounded below by Land claimed by Peter Amon & above by Vacant Land Which tract of Land has been occupied as required by Law

Opelousas 25th Dec 1813

> Etienne Aymond & Sophie Lemoine
>
> Marriage Contract - April 10, 1815

State of Louisiana

Parish of Avoyelles   No. 53

  Etienne Amon

    &   Contract of Marriage

  Sophie Lemoine

  Today, the tenth day of April year of our Grace, eighteen hundred fifteen of the independence of the United States of America,   Before me, Alexandre Plauche', Judge of the Parish of Avoyelles, Judge of the court, authorized by law to complete the functions of Notary Public, so in person and in presence of witnesses, the Sieur Etienne Amon, legitimate son and major of Mr. Jean Amon, father and Dame Marianne Joffrion, and Mademoiselle Sophie Lemoine, legitimate daughter of Mr. Guillaume Lemoine and Dame Guillaume Lemoine, Nei Marie Couvillon, with their consent of their father and mother, entered into marriage, both residents of the parish and consequently because of the marriage the Sieur Guillaume Lemoine gives to his daughter 4 arpents of land, found bordered by un cate (hill) by himself (Guillaume Lemoine) and by the other Mr. Joffrion, father, estimated at 700 piastres (dollars). Also a bed (garnie: meaning with decorations, etc.) estimated 64 piastres and one armoire of cypress, estimated 20. The said Sophie Lemoine brings to their community property, the following objects…she proves that she legally owns a "negrete" (black slave girl) by the name of Marguerite, 24 years old, a Creole (half white) and estimated 150 piastres .   Also, nine cows, and their calves, estimated $54, two _____ estimated 45 piastres, six young yearlings estimated 30 piastres, a young filly estimated at 12 piastres, a _____, sum of 380 piastres.

  Etienne Amon contributes to the community property 23 cows estimated $230 piastres, 34 young yearlings 170 piastres, 7 mares with colts estimated 136 paistres, 3 horses $65. A note from his brother Pierre Amon in the amount of $300, and said note to be paid on demand to Etienne, the whole sum being $900, written and prepared by law in my presence, Alexandre Plauche', Judge of Avoyelles Parish, accepted by Mr. Guillaume Lemoine, Sophie Lemoine, Marie Couvillon, Marianne Joffrion and Jean Aymond.

Witnesses		Signed Stephen Amon
D. Plissy	marque X	Sophie Lemoine
Bapt Andier	marque X	de Guillaume Lemoine
S. Touinier	marque X	de Jean Amon
V. LeDuc	marque X	De Marie Couvillon
	Marque X	De Marianne Joffrion

Before me: A. Plauche' Judge, Parish of Avoyelle

38

Certificate
No. 124

The United States of America,

To all to whom these presents shall come, Greeting:

Whereas, Stephen Aymond of the Parish of Avoyelles

has deposited in the General Land Office of the United States, a certificate of the Register of the Land Office at Opelousas,

whereby it appears that full payment has been made by the said Stephen Aymond

according to the provisions of the Act of Congress of the 24th of April, 1820, entitled "An act making further provision for the sale of the Public Lands;" for

the East half of the fractional South West quarter of fractional section twenty two, in Township One South of Range Four East, in the District

of Lands offered for Sale at Opelousas Louisiana, Containing Ninety four Acres and three hundredths of an Acre

according to the official plat of the survey of the said Lands, returned to the General Land Office by the Surveyor General, which said tract has been purchased by the said Stephen Aymond

NOW KNOW YE, That the **UNITED STATES OF AMERICA**, in consideration of the premises, and in conformity with the several acts of Congress, in such case made and provided, have Given and Granted, and, by these presents, do give and grant, unto the said Stephen Aymond and to his heirs the said tract above described: To Have and to Hold the same, together with all the rights, privileges, immunities and appurtenances, of whatsoever nature thereto belonging, unto the said Stephen Aymond and to his heirs and assigns forever.

In testimony whereof, I, John Quincy Adams

PRESIDENT OF THE UNITED STATES OF AMERICA, have caused these letters to be made Patent, and the seal of the General Land Office to be hereunto affixed.

Given under my hand, at the City of Washington, the tenth day of May — in the year of our Lord, one thousand eight hundred and twenty seven and of the Independence of the United States the

fifty first

By the President,

J. Q. A.

Commissioner of the General Land Office.

> Marriage contract between Stephen Aymond **and** Perrine Juneau
> August 24, 1829

Know all men by these present that Mr. Stephen Aymond as principal and Joseph Kimball as Security are held and firmly bound into the conversion of the State of Louisiana Successor in Office in the full sum of Five hundred dollars for the payment whereof we bind ourselves our things, administrators and ___ firmly by these present signed with our ___ and sealed with our seals this twenty fourth day of August one thousand eight hundred and twenty-nine.

Whereas the above bound in Stephen Aymond had appointed to the judge of the Parish to obtain a license to Contract marriage with Perrine Juneau.

Now therefore the functions of this obligation is just that if there arises no legal impediments to law marriage then and in such case the above obligation to ___ and void otherwise to remain in full force and virtue.

L.J. Barbin   S. Aymond   X   J.P. Kimball

Marriage of Etienne Stephen Aymond to Perrine Juneau

August 25, 1829

State of Louisiana

Parish of Avoyelles

Be it known that on this twenty-fifth day of August in the year of Our Lord One thousand eight hundred and twenty-nine

Lewis James Barbin Parish Judge in our for the Parish of Avoyelles have   to the do   of Stephen Aymond on Bayou Rouge, for the purpose of Celebrating the marriage agreed upon between him and Perrine Juneau, both of this parish and above age.

And then were there in the presence of Julien Deshautell, Joseph Kimball and S.   Riche witnesses thereto gives, after having taken the concerns of the parties to the judge have the Stephen Aymond and Perrine Juneau in the Holy bonds of matrimony.

In witness whoever they have hereunto see their   with   this day aforesaid Perine Juneau not knowing how to   has made her mark.

Joseph Kimble   S. Aymond

   Riche   Perrine X Juneau

   Julien Deshautell   Barbin

                                  Judge

> Sale of slave belonging to Sophie
> Lemoine by Stephen
>
> May 1, 1830

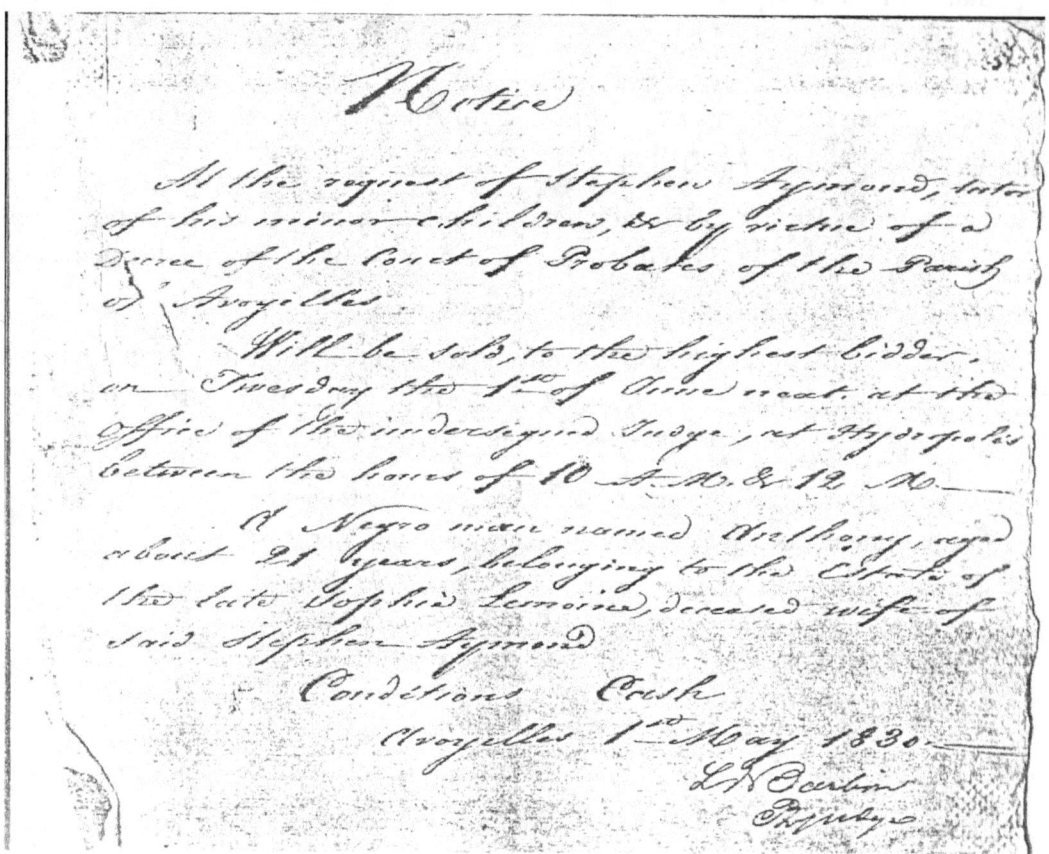

Notice

At the request of Stephen Aymond, tutor of the minor children by   of a decree of the Court of Probate of the Parish of Avoyelles.

Will be sold to the highest bidder on Tuesday the 1st of June   at the office of the Judge at Hydropolis between the hours of 10 A.M. and 12 noon.

A negro man named Anthony about 21 years, belonging to the estate of Sophie Lemoine, deceased wife of said Stephen Aymond.

Conditions   Cash

Avoyelles 1st May 1830

LN Barbin

Judge

Stephen Aymond
in the U.S. General Land Office Records, 1796-1907

Name:	Stephen Aymond
Issue Date:	3 Apr 1832
Acres:	141.2
Meridian:	Louisiana
State:	Louisiana
County:	Avoyelles
Township:	1-S
Range:	4-E
Section:	22
Accession Number:	LA1290___.247
Metes and Bounds:	No
Land Office:	Opelousas
Canceled:	No
US Reservations:	No
Mineral Reservations:	No
Authority:	April 24, 1820: Sale-Cash Entry (3 Stat. 566)
Document Number:	397

Source Information

Ancestry.com. *U.S. General Land Office Records, 1796-1907* [database on-line]. Provo, UT, USA: Ancestry.com Operations Inc, 2008.

Original data: United States. Bureau of Land Management, General Land Office Records. *Automated Records Project; Federal Land Patents, State Volumes.* http://www.glorecords.blm.gov/. Springfield, Virginia: Bureau of Land Management, Eastern States, 2007.

Description

This database contains land patents from 1796-1907 for 13 U.S. states. Information recorded in land patents includes: name of patentee, issue date, state of patent, acres of land, legal land description, authority under which the land was acquired, and other details relating to the land given. Learn more...

44

Louisiana > Avoyelles

Certificate
No. 397

The United States of America,

To all to whom these presents shall come, Greeting:

Whereas, Stephen Aymond, of the Parish of Avoyelles, Louisiana has deposited in the General Land Office of the United States, a certificate of the Register of the Land Office at Opelousas, whereby it appears that full payment has been made by the said Stephen Aymond, according to the provisions of the Act of Congress of the 24th of April, 1820, entitled "An act making further provision for the sale of the Public Lands," for the Lot numbered four, of section twenty five, in Township one South, thirty first degree, North Latitude, of range four East in the District of Lands subject to sale at Opelousas, Louisiana, containing one hundred and forty one acres and twenty hundredths of an acre, according to the official plat of the survey of the said Lands, returned to the General Land Office by the Surveyor General, which said tract has been purchased by the said Stephen Aymond.

NOW KNOW YE, That the **UNITED STATES OF AMERICA,** in consideration of the premises, and in conformity with the several acts of Congress, in such case made and provided, have Given and Granted, and, by these presents, do give and grant, unto the said Stephen Aymond, and to his heirs, — the said tract above described; To Have and to Hold the same, together with all the rights, privileges, immunities and appurtenances, of whatever nature thereto belonging, unto the said Stephen Aymond, and to his — heirs and assigns forever.

In testimony whereof, I, Andrew Jackson

PRESIDENT OF THE UNITED STATES OF AMERICA, have caused these letters to be made Patent, and the seal of the General Land Office to be hereunto affixed.

Given under my hand, at the city of Washington, the third day of April, — in the year of our Lord, one thousand eight hundred and thirty three, and of the Independence of the United States the fifty-sixth.

Signed March 25 1833

By the President, Andrew Jackson

By A.J. Donelson Secy

Elijah Hayward Commissioner of the General Land Office.

215 of 1297

45

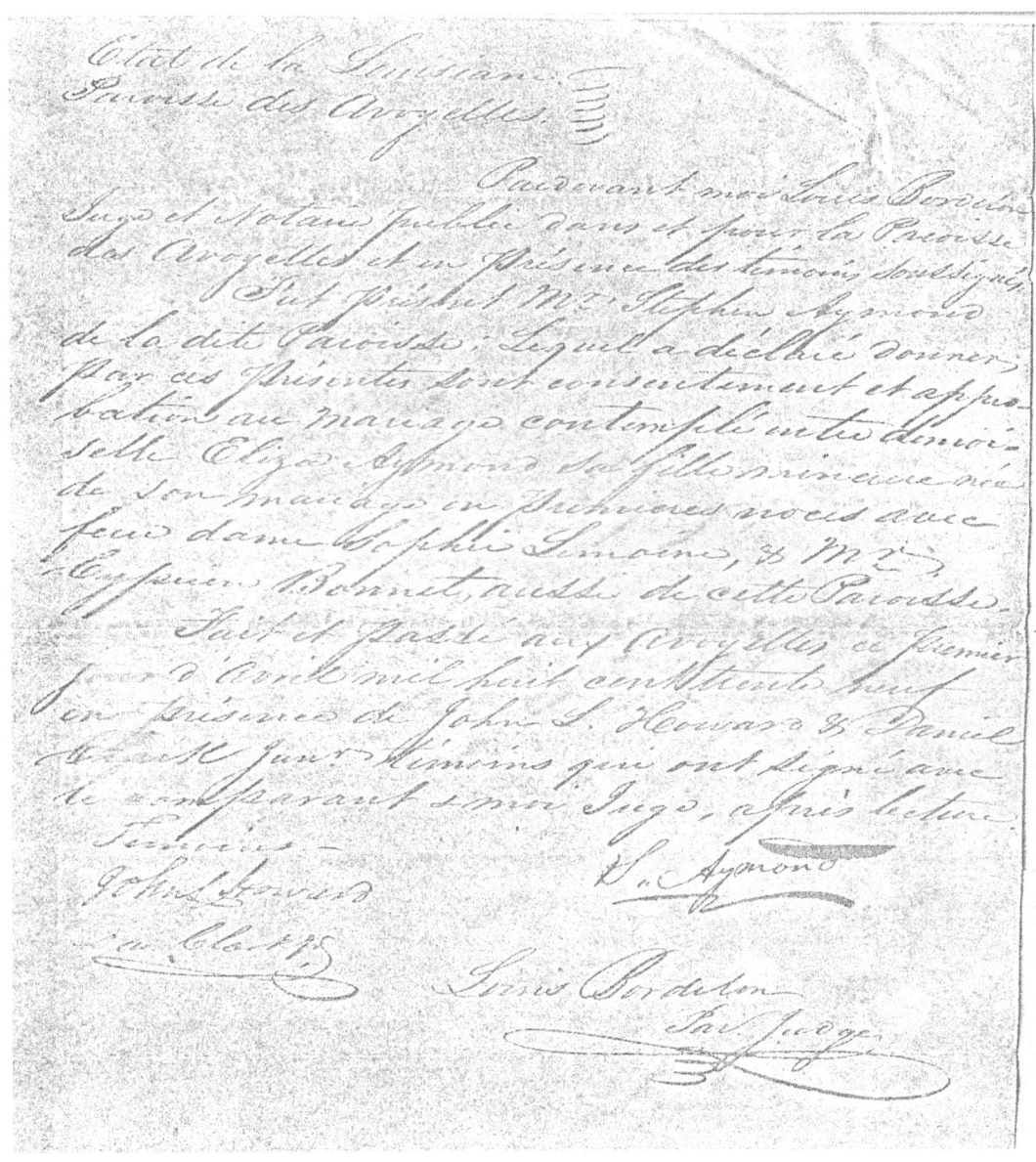

Marriage of Eliza Aymond and Cyprien Bonnet
April 1, 1839

État de la Louisiane
Paroisse des Avoyelles

   L'an mil huit cent trente
neuf, le premier jour du mois d'Avril, en la
Paroisse des Avoyelles et au domicile du sieur
Stephen Aymond, par devant moi Louis Bordelon
Juge de la dite Paroisse, en présence des témoins
soussignés. Sont personnellement comparus,
Mr Cyprien Bonnet fils mineur du sieur
Jean Bonnet & de dame Françoise Gaspard
son épouse, d'une part, et Mademoiselle
Eliza Aymond fille mineure du sieur
Stephen Aymond & de feue dame Sophie
Lemoine sa épouse en premières noces, d'autre
part, tous deux demeurant en la dite
Paroisse; Lesquels ont été par moi légiti-
mement mariés à leur requête & après
avoir rempli à cet effet les formalités
de la loi.—

   En foi de quoi ils ont signé en
présence des témoins & Juge soussignés;
le sieur Cyprien Bonnet par sa marque
ordinaire, ne sachant pas écrire.—

Témoins —
John L. Konrad
Jean Chastés &c
A. Latham

Cyprien + Bonnet
   marque
Eleyea Aymond

47

Permission to Marry
Permission for Caroline Aymond, daughter of
Etienne and Sophie to marry
Zenon Areaux
October 13, 1840

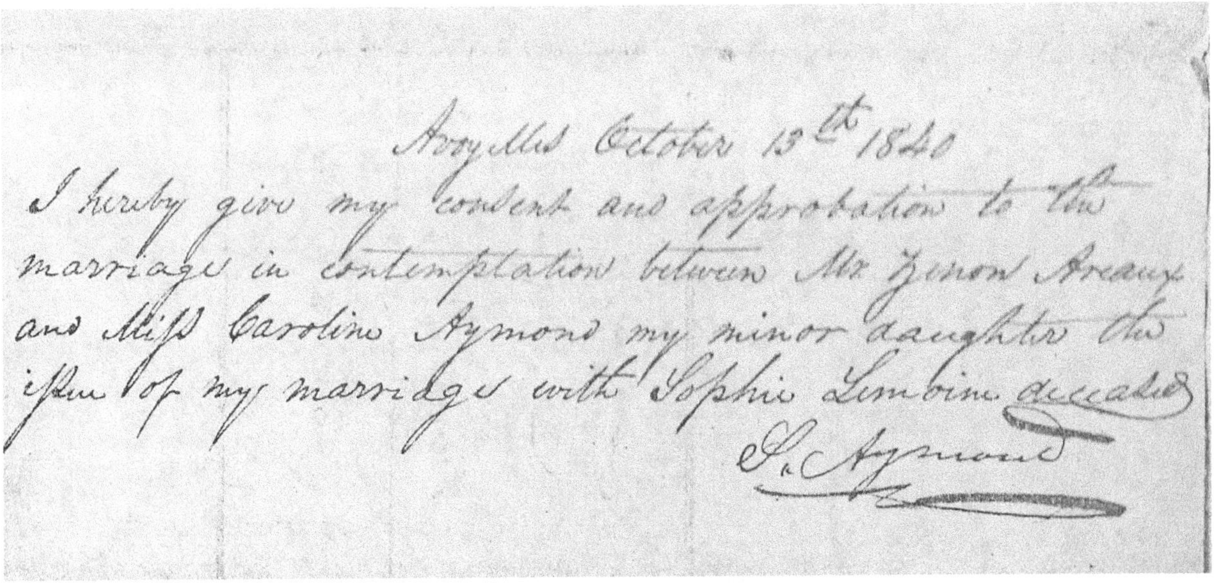

Avoyelles October 13th 1840

I hereby give my consent and approbation to the marriage in contemplation between Mr Zenon Areaux and Miss Caroline Aymond my minor daughter the issue of my marriage with Sophie Lemoine deceased

E. Aymond

Marriage of Caroline Aymond and

Zenon Areaux

State of Louisiana) Be it known that on this thirtenth
Parish of Avoyelles) day of October Anno Domini eighteen
hundred and forty

Before me Gervais Baillio Parish Judge
in and for the Parish aforesaid and in presence of the
witnesses hereinafter named and undersigned

Personally came and appeared Mr Zenon Areaux
of the one part and Miss Caroline Aymond of the other
part both inhabitants of this Parish who having complied
with the formalities made and required in such cases
were by me at their request united in the Holy Estate
of Matrimony –

In testimony whereof the said appearers
have hereunto affixed their names at the domicil of
Stephen Aymond on Bayou Rouge in this Parish
in presence of Messrs. Eledzar G. Paxton, Richard W. Ray
and Robert L. Taliaferro witnesses of full age and domi=
=ciliated in this Parish who have signed with the
said appearers and me Judge after lecture.
The lady appearer having declared that she does not
know how to write has signed by making her mark
"ordinaire". The whole done and signed on the day and
year and at the place aforesaid

Witnesses

E. G. Paxton

R. W. Ray

R L Taliaferro

Zenon Areaux
and
Caroline Aymond – dau of Etienne Aymond
& Sophie Lemoine

Y. Areaux

her
Caroline + Aymond
mark

Gervais Baillio Par
Judge

49

ancestry

Stephen Aymond
in the 1840 United States Federal Census

Name:	Stephen Aymond
Home in 1840 (City, County, State):	Avoyelles, Louisiana
Free White Persons - Males - Under 5:	2
Free White Persons - Males - 5 thru 9:	1
Free White Persons - Males - 10 thru 14:	3
Free White Persons - Males - 15 thru 19:	1
Free White Persons - Males - 40 thru 49:	1
Free White Persons - Females - Under 5:	1
Free White Persons - Females - 5 thru 9:	3
Free White Persons - Females - 10 thru 14:	2
Free White Persons - Females - 30 thru 39:	1
Slaves - Males - Under 10:	3
Slaves - Males - 10 thru 23:	4
Slaves - Males - 24 thru 35:	3
Slaves - Males - 36 thru 54:	1
Slaves - Females - Under 10:	3
Slaves - Females - 10 thru 23:	4
Slaves - Females - 24 thru 35:	4
Free White Persons - Under 20:	13
Free White Persons - 20 thru 49:	2
Total Free White Persons:	15
Total Slaves:	22
Total All Persons - Free White, Free Colored, Slaves:	37

Source Citation
Year: 1840; Census Place: Avoyelles, Louisiana; Roll: 128; Page: 291; Image: 594; Family History Library Film: 0009689

Source Information
Ancestry.com. 1840 United States Federal Census [database on-line]. Provo, UT, USA: Ancestry.com Operations, Inc., 2010.
Images reproduced by FamilySearch.

Original data: Sixth Census of the United States, 1840. (NARA microfilm publication M704, 580 rolls). Records of the Bureau of the Census, Record Group 29. National Archives, Washington, D.C.

Description

⊲‖ancestry

Stephen Aymond
in the U.S. General Land Office Records, 1796-1907

Name:	Stephen Aymond
Issue Date:	10 Apr 1843
Acres:	80.4
Meridian:	Louisiana
State:	Louisiana
County:	Avoyelles
Township:	3-N
Range:	3-E
Section:	18
Accession Number:	LA0960___.229
Metes and Bounds:	No
Land Office:	Ouachita
Canceled:	No
US Reservations:	No
Mineral Reservations:	No
Authority:	April 24, 1820: Sale-Cash Entry (3 Stat. 566)
Document Number:	5665

Source Information

Ancestry.com. *U.S. General Land Office Records, 1796-1907* [database on-line]. Provo, UT, USA: Ancestry.com Operations Inc, 2008.

Original data: United States. Bureau of Land Management, General Land Office Records. *Automated Records Project; Federal Land Patents, State Volumes.* http://www.glorecords.blm.gov/. Springfield, Virginia: Bureau of Land Management, Eastern States, 2007.

Description

This database contains land patents from 1796-1907 for 13 U.S. states. Information recorded in land patents includes: name of patentee, issue date, state of patent, acres of land, legal land description, authority under which the land was acquired, and other details relating to the land given. Learn more...

Jean buys 80.45 acres of property

April 10, 1843

THE UNITED STATES OF AMERICA,

CERTIFICATE No. 5665

To all to whom these Presents shall come, Greeting:

WHEREAS *Stephen Aymond, of Avoyelles, Louisiana*

has deposited in the GENERAL LAND OFFICE of the United States, a Certificate of the REGISTER OF THE LAND OFFICE at *Ouachita* whereby it appears that full payment has been made by the said

Stephen Aymond according to the provisions of the Act of Congress of the 24th of April, 1820, entitled "An Act making further provision for the sale of the Public Lands," for *the East half of the South East quarter of Section eighteen, in Township three, of Range three East, in the District of Lands subject to sale at Ouachita, Louisiana, containing eighty acres and forty hundredths of an acre,*

according to the official plat of the survey of the said Lands, returned to the General Land Office by the SURVEYOR GENERAL, which said tract has been purchased by the said *Stephen Aymond,*

NOW KNOW YE, That the United States of America, in consideration of the Premises, and in conformity with the several acts of Congress, in such case made and provided, HAVE GIVEN AND GRANTED, and by these presents DO GIVE AND GRANT, unto the said *Stephen Aymond,*

and to *his* heirs, the said tract above described: TO HAVE AND TO HOLD the same, together with all the rights, privileges, immunities, and appurtenances of whatsoever nature, thereunto belonging, unto the said

Stephen Aymond, and to *his* heirs and assigns forever.

In Testimony Whereof, I, *John Tyler* PRESIDENT OF THE UNITED STATES OF AMERICA, have caused these Letters to be made PATENT, and the SEAL of the GENERAL LAND OFFICE to be hereunto affixed.

GIVEN under my hand, at the CITY OF WASHINGTON, the *tenth* day of *April* in the Year of our Lord one thousand eight hundred and *forty three* and of the INDEPENDENCE OF THE UNITED STATES the Sixty *Seventh.*

[L.S.]

BY THE PRESIDENT: *John Tyler*

By *R. Tyler* Sec'y.

J. Williamson RECORDER of the General Land Office.

Heirs of   Mrs. Stephen Aymond
Partition   27th August 1846
State of Louisiana
Parish of Avoyelles

Be it known that on this twenty seventh day of August year eighteen hundred forty six before me Gervaid Pzaillio Parish Judge and officio notary public and for the Parish and state aforesaid in presence of the witnesses hereinafter named and undersigned personally came and appears Stephen Aymond, Jr. and Jean Baptiste Aymond, Peter Aymond, William Aymond, Mrs. Aliza Aymond wife of Cyprien Bonnet, by him herein duly and authorizes Mrs.   Caroline Aymond wife   of Zenon Arceaux by him herein duly aides authorizes and   Mrs. Sophie Aymond wife of Nichol Nicholson by him herein duly aids,   authorizes and   all   of the parish and state aforesaid which   appeared seven in number   of the only children   and heirs of Mrs. Sophie Lemoine deceased the   espouse of her marriage with Stephen   Aymond declared that whereas they wish to make a partition and division of the property and   effects rights and credits belonging to them in common and which   to them from the   estate of their deceased mother the said Sophie Lemoine and   partly of the separate property oftheir deceased mother and partly of her share in the community   property   gains that separate between her and her surviving husband the said Stephen Aymond   partly from the Estate of her grandmother Marie Couvillion deceased wife of Guillaume Lemoine   of their grandfather Guillaume Lemoine and partly of a money judgment   which they there appear obtained against their father and natural tutor the said Stephen   Aymond and by notorial deeds and   sales from their said father

1) Stephen Aymond, Jr. takes as his share and portion following:
   a. The slave Joachion 19 years, $600;
   b. Edmond, 7 years, $260;
   c.   Undivided one-half of the parcels of land south half of NW quarter and the NE quarter of the NW quarter of the NW quarter of section W 10 in township "wone" South of Range W 3 East in the South western District of State of Louisiana
   d. 159 84/100 acres it continues with 3 parcels

2) Jean Baptiste

   a. Slave Joe, 15 years, $1500;
   b. Henry, $260;
   c. Undivided ½ of property

3) Eliza, wife of Cyprien Bonnett:

    d.   Clarisse, yellow girl, 15 years old, $600

    e.   Eliza, 6 years old, $220

    f.   Jenny, Negro woman, 35 years old, $225.

4)   Caroline, wife of Zenon Arceaux

    a.   Slave, Manette, $525

    b.   Slave, Sudan, 35 years old, $350.

    c.   80 acres undivided, ¼ Pointe Mayre, the other half to Stephen, $50.

5)   Peter Aymond

    a.   Charles "Griff", $550.

    b.   Slave "Hetty", Negro girl 4 years old, $220.

    c.   Slave "William", 7 years old, $260

    d.   78 and 21/100 acres in indursion to be taken out of the lot no. four in Section no. 22 in township W one South Range, No. 4, East, valued at $350. Total $1350.

6)   Mrs. Sophie Aymond wife of Nichol Nicholson takes for her portion and there is allotted other the following described property at the price offered.

    a.   Slave Margaret, 35 years old and child Sarah, 2 year old girl., $700.

    b.   Slave Azelie, griffe girl, child of Margaret, valued at $350.

    c.   78 and 41/100 acres of land to be taken from front and western extreme of the east half of the fractional SW quarter of fractional section 22 in Township one South of Range four east in the District of lands offered for sale at Opelousas, LA, $450. Total $1500.

7)   William Aymond takes for his share and portions

    a.   Slave Jacob, 8 years old, $450.

    b.   Slave Sarah, 40 years old, griffe, $500.

    c.   78 and 21/100 acres of land as follows: 15 and 62/100 acres near or Southern extremity of east half of the fractional section SW quarter of fractional section 22 in township on South of Range 4 East and 62 tobe taken in division out of the lot W four in Section W 22 Township W one Range W4 E , $400.

54

ancestry

Stephen Aymond
in the 1850 United States Federal Census

Name:	Stephen Aymond
Age:	53
Birth Year:	abt 1797
Birthplace:	Louisiana
Home in 1850:	Avoyelles, Louisiana, USA
Gender:	Male
Family Number:	693

Household Members:

Name	Age
Stephen Aymond	53
Perina Aymond	40
Joseph Aymond	16
Valentin Aymond	16
Milia Aymond	12
Prudent Aymond	10
Prudence Aymond	10
Gervais Aymond	8
Oline Aymond	6
Oline Aymond	6
Azelia Aymond	0
Sophie Aymond	22
John Aymond	1

Source Citation

Year: *1850*; Census Place: *Avoyelles, Louisiana*; Roll: *M432_229*; Page: *148B*; Image: *301*

Source Information

Ancestry.com. *1850 United States Federal Census* [database on-line]. Provo, UT, USA: Ancestry.com Operations, Inc., 2009.
Images reproduced by FamilySearch.

Original data: Seventh Census of the United States, 1850; (National Archives Microfilm Publication M432, 1009 rolls); Records of
the Bureau of the Census, Record Group 29; National Archives, Washington, D.C.

Description

This database is an index to individuals enumerated in the 1850 United States Federal Census, the Seventh Census of the
United States. Census takers recorded many details including each person's name, age as of the census day, sex, color;
birthplace, occupation of males over age fifteen, and more. No relationships were shown between members of a household.
Additionally, the names of those listed on the population schedule are linked to actual images of the 1850 Federal Census.
Learn more...

Marriage of Paul Zenon Ducote and Sophie Aymond, daughter of Stephen and Sophie Aymond. Their marriage took place at the home of Doctor Defosse's home, which still stands in Mansura, LA and is on the National Register. Note the addition of the letters "y" and "d" on the "Aymond" name. Also, Paul and Sophie Aymond Ducote later became the parents of Odelia Ducote who married Theophile Descant, grandparents of Ordean Gaspard Aymond

May 2, 1854

State of Louisiana

Parish of Avoyelles

Be it remembered, that on the 2ⁿᵈ day of May, A.D. 1854 Paul Zenon Ducote and Mrs. Sophie Aymond widow of N. Nicholson, both residents of the parish aforesaid, at the domicile of Doct Defossee in the said parish personally appeared before me, Joseph Cappel, on   the Justice of the peace in and for the parish of Avoyelles, together with M. M. Matthews ___ Descant Theo A Dupuy witnesses of full age and resident in the said parish, and that then and there   the said Paul Zenon Ducote and Sophie Aymond having produced the license required by law, signified their desire and intention, before us the said justice and witnesses to be united in the estate of matrimony, whereupon, after the proclamation made, and no impediment, being suggested they the said Paul Zenon Ducote and Sophie Aymond were by me, the said justice, in the presence of said witnesses joined in wedlock according to the laws of the State of Louisiana and duly pronounced to be the husband and wife. In testimony, whereof, the parties to the said marriage hereunto affix their signature by making their ordinary marks together with me the said justice, and the aforesaid witnesses on this 2ⁿᵈ day of May A.D., 1854 at the domicile of Doct Defossee in the parish aforesaid.

Witnesses

M M Matthews

___ Descant

T.A. Dupuy

his

Paul Zenon x Ducote
mark

her

Sophie x Aymond
mark

Joseph Cappel

Justice of Peace

Marriage of Sophie Aymond, daughter of Etienne and Sophie Lemoine

Sophie married Paul "Zenon" Ducote, known as "Degastille" on May 2, 1854. Her marriage took place at the Defosse home, which still stands in Mansura, Louisiana and is on the National Register. She was later to become the mother of Odelia Ducote (m. Theophile Descant) who was Ordean Gaspard Aymond's

1860 United States Federal Census

Name:	**Stephen Aymond**
Age in 1860:	64
Birth Year:	abt 1796
Birthplace:	Louisiana
Home in 1860:	Avoyelles, Louisiana
Gender:	Male
Post Office:	Marksville
Value of real estate:	

Household Members:	Name	Age
	Stephen Aymond	64
	Perine Aymond	50
	Prudence Aymond	17
	Auline Aymond	14
	Aulin Aymond	14

Source Citation: Year: *1860*; Census Place: *, Avoyelles, Louisiana*; Roll: *M653_407*; Page: *360*; Image: *360*; Family History Library Film: *803407*.

Source Information:

Ancestry.com. *1860 United States Federal Census* [database on-line]. Provo, UT, USA: Ancestry.com Operations, Inc., 2009. Images reproduced by FamilySearch.

Original data: 1860 U.S. census, population schedule. NARA microfilm publication M653, 1,438 rolls. Washington, D.C.: National Archives and Records Administration, n.d.

Description:
This database is an index to individuals enumerated in the 1860 United States Federal Census, the Eighth Census of the United States. Census takers recorded many details including each person's name, age as of the census day, sex, color; birthplace, occupation of males over age fifteen, and more. No relationships were shown between members of a household. Additionally, the names of those listed on the population schedule are linked to actual images of the 1860 Federal Census.

58

District Court Parish of Avoyelles
State of Louisiana

Succession of
Stephen Aymond
dec.

I Perrine Juneau do solemnly swear, that I will well and truly discharge and perform all the duties incumbent on me, as natural tutorix of Germaine Prudence, Oline & Olin Aymond minor children issue of my marriage with Stephen Aymond deceased to the best of my ability and according to law. So help me God.
Sworn to and subscribed before me,
This 10th day of January 1862.

Z.G. Riche'
Justice of the Peace

Joseph Aymond as tutor of the
children of Stephen Aymond

Succession of
Stephen Aymond dec
Oath of under tutor
Filed 13th January 1862

District Court…Parish of Avoyelles
-State of Louisiana-

Succession of
____
Stephen Aymond
dec

I, Joseph Aymond do solemnly
swear, that I will well and truly
discharge and preform all the duties
encumbered on me, as under tutor
of Germaine, Prudence, Oline, and
Olin Aymond, minor children of Stephen Aymond
Deceased, and Perine Juneau, to the best of my
Ability and according to law, So help me God
Sworn to and subscribed before me, Joseph Aymond
This 10th January 1862.
Z.G. Riche
Justice of the Peace

Petition for family meeting

January 23, 1867

Suc of Sophie
Aymond decd.
Petition for family
meeting
Filed 25th Jan 1867

To the Hon. The Judge of this 7th Judicial District, holding Court
In and for the Parish of Avoyelles, Louisiana.
The petition of Zenon Areaux a resident of your parish and
state, most respectfully represents;   That he is the admin-
istrator of the Estate of Sophie Aymond deceased widow of
Degastile Ducote – and that there are several minor child-
Ren: Gustave, Arstide, Ophelia, Joseph, Oscar, Augustine
& Odelia, issue of the deceased marriage to whom as yet
No tutor, have been appointed. He represents that in
Order to appoint to said minors, tutors it is necessary that
        A family meeting should be convened. Wherefore he pray
that an order issue to Alfred H Bordelon not. pub. (notary public)
commanding and empowering him to convoke a family meeting
composed of Jean Baptiste, Prudent Aymond, Martin Lacombe,
Cevert Chenevert, and William Laborde, nearest relatives
Or in default of same of friends to appoint
tutors to the minors; Gustave, Arstide, Ophelia, Joseph,
Oscar, Augustine & Odelia Ducote, issue of the marriage
of Degastile Ducote and Sophie Aymond both
decd. and for all such further orders and decries
as may be necessary in the
                                deceased wife Marcellia
Kohen be sold for cash at public auction to the highest & last
Bidder after all the legal advertisements and to that effect
Let a commission issue to Edmard de Gesseris public auctioneer.
Clerks' office, Avoyelles this 23rd. day of January
A.D. 1867
                        F.F. Goudeau

Petition for family meeting

January 23, 1867

A.D. 1867 Nov 15, 1979   By: Ordeon Goofard ———————————
Aymond – Great – Granddaughter of
Sophie Aymond

Succ of Sophie
Aymond dec'd
Petition for family
meeting
Filed 25th Jan, 1867

To the Hon. the Judge of the 7th Judicial District, holding Court
in and for the Parish of Avoyelles, Louisiana.

The petition of Zénon Aucoin a resident of your parish and
State, most respectfully represents: That he is the administrator of the Estate of Sophie Aymond deceased widow of
Dégastile Ducôté— And that there are several minor children viz, Gustave, Aristide, Ophélia Joseph Oscar, Augustin
& Odélia, issue of the deceased marriage to whom as yet
no tutors have been appointed. He represents that in
order to appoint to said minors, tutors it is necessary that
a family meeting should be convoked.   Wherefore he prays
that an order issue to Alfred H. Bordelon Not pub. Commanding and impowering him to convoke a family meeting composed of Jno Baptiste Aymond, Prudent Aymond,
Martin Lacombe, Evarist Chenraet & William Laborde
nearest relatives or in default of same of friends to appoint tutors to the minors Gustave, Aristide, Ophélia,
Joseph, Oscar, Augustin & Odélia Ducôté, issue of the
marriage of Dégastile Ducôté & Sophie Aymond both
dec'd and for all such further orders and decrees as may be necessary in the

Same copy
By Ordeon Goofard
Aymond
Nov 15, 1979

Return he sold for Cash at public auction to the highest & last
bidder after all the legal advertisements and to that effect
let a commission issue to Edward de Genères public auctioneer.
Clerk's office, Avoyelles this 23rd day of January
A.D. 1867
                                        F. F. Goudeau Clk.

Succession of Sophie Aymond

February 2, 1867

Suc. Of Sophie Aymond, decd.

Petition for sale

Filed 2 Feb. 1867

To the Hon. W. Cooley, Judge of the 7th Judicial District of La holding sessions in for Avoyelles Parish.

The petition of Zenon Arceaux, a resident of your Parish and State most respectfully represents. That he is the administrator of the succession of Sophie Aymond dec and that said succession is greatly in debt and that in order to effect the settlement of the affairs of said Estate it becomes necessary that a sale of the property belonging to it should take place.

Wherefore; he prays that an order issue to J. J. Ducote Sheriff and ex-officio Public auctioneer in and for the Parish of Avoyelles, commanding and empowering him to sell at public auction after the legal advertisements, all the property as per inventory belonging to said Succession upon the following terms and conditions. The moveable property for cash, the immovable property, as follows, one half payable on the 1st of April A.D. 1869. Purchases furnishing their notes with two good and solvent securities in solido to the order and satisfaction of the administrator, the lands to remain specially mortgaged and vendors privilege retained, until full and final payment of the principal and interest. He further prays for all such further orders and decrees as may be necessary in the premises and for general relief.

L. J. Ducote

Atty. For Pet.

Let a sale of the property belonging to the succession of Sophie Aymond decd. be made upon the terms and conditions as prayed for in the foregoing petition, and that a commission issue accordingly directed to the sheriff of this Parish.

Clerk's Office Avoyelles, this second

Day of February A.D. 1867 (or 1869?)   J. J. Goudeau, ___

Succession of Sophie Aymond

February 2, 1867

To the Hon. W. H. Cooley Judge of the Judge 7th Judicial District of La. holding sessions in & for Avoyelles Parish.

The petition of Zenon Ayreaux, a resident of your Parish & State Most respectfully represents. That he is the administrator of the succession of Sophie Aymond dec? and that said succession is greatly in debt and that in order to effect the settlement of the affairs of said Estate it becomes necessary that a sale of the property belonging to it should take place.

Wherefore; he prays that an order issue to J. J. Ducote Sheriff and ex-officio Public auctioneer, in and for the Parish of Avoyelles, commanding and empowering him to sell at public auction after the legal advertisements, all the property as per inventory belonging to said Succession upon the following terms and conditions, viz the movable property for Cash, the immovable property, as follows, One half payable on the 1st of April A.D. 1868, the other half on the 1st of April A.D. 1869, Purchasers furnishing their notes with two good and solvent securities in solido to the order and satisfaction of the administrator, the

Chapter 5: Etienne Aymond, II and Elodie Chenevert

Etienne, II was born on April 24, 1816 at Point Magre, LA in Avoyelles Parish. He was the first of seven children born to Sophie, age 21 and Etienne, age 18. Etienne, II was baptized on December 7, 1817 when he was about one and a half years old.   On December 5, 1844, at the age of 28, Etienne II married Elodie Chenevert at Point Mezre. Elodie Chenevert was the daughter of Marcellin Chenevert and Eloise Baron.

Etienne Aymond, II died on June 15, 1868 at the age of fifty-two in the town of Moreauville, LA. His succession was filed before September 1870. On December 12, 1870, Elodie Chenevert filed a petition to be the natural tutrex of her two minor children, Irma and Stephen Ferrier. At that time, she had already married her second husband, Jean Baptiste Rabalais. In Inventory Book H at the Marksville Courthouse, the home of Jean Baptiste Rabalais, Jr. was listed as the location for the succession of Etienne Aymond on September 1870. Listed in the succession was 400 acres of land, one-half mile from "Bayou Jack" (near Dupont) with all buildings and improvements for $2,000. They also listed 80 acres at Point Maigre for $100.00, 6 head of cattle for $45.00 and one Creole mare for $15.00. This totaled $2215.50 (pots and pans, etc. included)!

Husband: Etienne Aymond II
DOB: April 24, 1816, Point Magre, LA
DOD: June 15, 1868, Moreauville
Buried:

Married: December 5, 1844 Point Mezre

Parents: Etienne "Stephen" Aymond (1797-1861)
    Sophie Lemoine (1794-1828)

Wife: Elodie Chenevert
DOB: 1824
DOD: 1905
 Father: Marcelin Chenevert
    (1792 -)
 Mother: Eloise Baron
    (1801-)

Children of Etienne and Elodie

Name	DOB –Marriage - DOD	Married	Notes
Marie Louise	DOB: 1845 M: 5/4/1862 M: 3/29/1869	Hildevert Juneau Charles Mason	Book B3, P. 176 Married in Etienne's home
Marcellin Aymond	DOB: 5/30/1849 in Plaucheville M: 1/9/1873 M: 9/20/1875 DOD: 5/11/1888 in Plaucheville	Irene (Irma) Firmin Olivia Dupuis DOB: 12/3/1850 Buried in Pineville	Marcellin & Irene Marriage: Book C, Page 486 Olivia was the daughter of Theodore A. Dupuy and Zoe Scallan.
Virginia Aymond	DOB: 1851 M: 10/16/1866	Joseph Marcotte	Book B3, Page 336 Succession of Joseph Marcotte: Book G, Page 9 Joseph was the son of Salluste Marcotte and Elizabeth Dillahunt
Irma Azelia Aymond	DOB: 1853 M: 12/28/1870	Euclide Firmin	
Stephen F. Aymond	DOB: 9/8/1859 M: 1/15/1880	Bazilize Firmin	Book D, Page 610
Notes: Elodie Chenevert remarried Jean Baptiste Rabalais on 9/22/1870 (Book C, p. 259)			

Consent of Parents Marcelin Chenevert and Eloise Baron for
the marriage of their daughter Eloise Chenevert to Etienne
Aymond, II. November 1844

Marriage License for
Etienne Aymond and Elodie Chenevert
December 5, 1844

State of Louisiana

Parish of Avoyelles

Know all men by their presence   that we Etienne Aymond and principal and
Charles Cappel _____ as security both of the parish of Avoyelles are held and bound
unto Mouton Governor of the State of Louisiana and his succe   in office in the sum
of five hundred dollars for   the payment whereof well and truly to be made we bind
ourselves and heirs,   , administration   and assigned firmly by these present,
signed with our hand at the parish of Avoyelles on this fifth day of December
A.D. eighteen hundred and forty-four.

The condition of the above obligation is such that whereas the above bounded
Etienne Aymond has this day applies to the undersigned parish judge for
license of marriage with Elodie Chenevert also of the parish of Avoyelles.

Now therefore if there shall hereafter appear to exist no legal impairment to
the said marriage then the above obligation to be null and void otherwise to remain in
full force and effect.

Signed and delivered in presence of the undersigned witnesses.

Etienne Aymond

Charles Cappel

1850 Census

69

ancestry

1850 United States Federal Census

Name:	**Etienne Aymond**
Age:	34
Birth Year:	abt 1816
Birthplace:	Louisiana
Home in 1850:	Avoyelles, Louisiana
Gender:	Male
Family Number:	719

Household Members:	Name	Age
	Etienne Aymond	34
	Elodie Aymond	23
	Marie Louise	5
	Marcel Louise	1

Source Citation: Year: *1850*; Census Place: , *Avoyelles, Louisiana*; Roll: *M432_229*; Page: *150A*; Image: *304*.

Source Information:

THE NATIONAL ARCHIVES ARCHIVES.GOV

Ancestry.com. *1850 United States Federal Census* [database on-line]. Provo, UT, USA: Ancestry.com Operations, Inc., 2009. Images reproduced by FamilySearch.

Original data: Seventh Census of the United States, 1850; (National Archives Microfilm Publication M432, 1009 rolls); Records of the Bureau of the Census, Record Group 29; National Archives, Washington, D.C.

Description:
This database is an index to individuals enumerated in the 1850 United States Federal Census, the Seventh Census of the United States. Census takers recorded many details including each person's name, age as of the census day, sex, color; birthplace, occupation of males over age fifteen, and more. No relationships were shown between members of a household. Additionally, the names of those listed on the population schedule are linked to actual images of the 1850 Federal Census.

© 2013, The Generations Network, Inc.

70

1860 United States Federal Census

Name:	**Etienne Aymond**
Age in 1860:	44
Birth Year:	abt 1816
Birthplace:	Louisiana
Home in 1860:	Avoyelles, Louisiana
Gender:	Male
Post Office:	Marksville
Value of real estate:	

Household Members:	Name	Age
	Etienne Aymond	44
	Elodie Aymond	36
	Marie Aymond	15
	Marcelin Aymond	10
	Virginie Aymond	8
	Irma Aymond	7
	Stephen Aymond	1

Source Citation: Year: *1860*; Census Place: *, Avoyelles, Louisiana*; Roll: *M653_407*; Page: *361*; Image: *361*; Family History Library Film: *803407*.

Source Information:

Ancestry.com. *1860 United States Federal Census* [database on-line]. Provo, UT, USA: Ancestry.com Operations, Inc., 2009. Images reproduced by FamilySearch.

Original data: 1860 U.S. census, population schedule. NARA microfilm publication M653, 1,438 rolls. Washington, D.C.: National Archives and Records Administration, n.d.

Description:
This database is an index to individuals enumerated in the 1860 United States Federal Census, the Eighth Census of the United States. Census takers recorded many details including each person's name, age as of the census day, sex, color; birthplace, occupation of males over age fifteen, and more. No relationships were shown between members of a household. Additionally, the names of those listed on the population schedule are linked to actual images of the 1860 Federal Census.

© 2013, The Generations Network, Inc.

1860 Census

72

Etienne Aymond
in the Louisiana, Wills and Probate Records, 1756-1984

Name:	Etienne Aymond
Probate Date:	15 Sep 1870
Probate Place:	Avoyelles, Louisiana, USA
Inferred Death Year:	Abt 1870
Inferred Death Place:	Louisiana, USA
Item Description:	Oaths and Bonds of Tutor Administration, Vol B, 1864-1871

Source Citation

Oaths and Bonds of Administration, 1855-1889; Author: *Avoyelles Parish (Louisiana). Clerk of Court*; Probate Place: *Avoyelles, Louisiana*

Source Information

Ancestry.com. *Louisiana, Wills and Probate Records, 1756-1984* [database on-line]. Provo, UT, USA: Ancestry.com Operations, Inc., 2015.

Original data: Louisiana County, District and Probate Courts.

Description

These probates from the state of Louisiana, 1756-1984, can bequeath a wealth of personal details on the decedent and other family members. Learn more...

© 2016, Ancestry.com

```
Oath of Under Tutor

Sept. 15, 1870
```

Suc of Parish Court   Parish of Avoyelles

Etienne Aymond   State of Louisiana

      decd.   Succession of

Oath of Under   Etienne Aymond   I Edmond Dufour do solemnly swear,
Tutor   that I will well and truly discharge and perform all the

Duties incumbered on me, as Under Tutor

of Irma and Stephen Ferrier Aymond minor children of Etienne

Aymond deceased and Elodie Chenevert, to the best of my ability and

according to law so help me God

sworn to and subscribed, Edmond Dufour

before me, this 15th day of

September 1870

                I.A. Morrow   dy clk.

74

Certificated of Natural Tutrix

Sept. 15, 1870

Succ of   Parish Court, Parish of Avoyelles

Etienne   State of Louisiana

Aymond decd.

Oath of Nat.   Succession of

Tutor   Etienne Aymond   I Elodie Chenevert do solemnly
Filed 15th   swear that I will well and truly

Sept 1870   discharge and perform all the duties incumbent on me as

Natural Tutrix of Irma and Stephen Ferrier Aymond minor

Children of my marriage with Etienne Aymond decd. To

the best of my ability and according to law so help me

God.

Sworn to and subscribed before me

This 15th day of Sept 1870.   Elodie X Chenevert

F.   Ricord dy clk

75

Louisiana, Wills and Probate Records, 1756-1984 for Etienne Aymond

Succ of

Etienne Aymond	State of Louisiana
Decd.	Parish of Avoyelles
Certificate of the Recorder Filed Sept. 15, 1870	

I do hereby certify that Mrs. Elodie Chenevert has in this day duly filed in m my office A certificate from the Clerk of the Court of this parish whereby it appears that the Inventory of the property belonging to the Succession of Etienne Aymond decd. filed in his office that the said inventory amounts to the sum of two thousand two hundred and fifteen dollars which said amount is confided to the Administration of the said Elodie Chenevert as Natural Tutrix of Irma and Stephen Aymond, the issue of her marriage with Etienne Aymond decd.

Given under my hand and seal of office at Marksville, Avoyelles this 15th day of September AD 1870

L.V. Gremillion

Recorder

Succession of Etienne Aymond

December 7, 1870

Suc of

Etienne Aymond
decd.
Petition to

Hold fam meet
Fixing terms of
same
Filed Dec 1870

To the Honorable the judge of the Parish Court sitting in and for the Parish of Avoyelles, State of Louisiana.

The petition of Mrs. Elodie Chenevert, wife of Jean B. Rabalais, Jr. and him duly aided authorized and assisted as resident of the Parish of Avoyelles with respect shows that as natural tutrix of Irma and Stephen Ferrier Aymond, minor children, the issue of her marriage with her first husband, Etienne Aymond, deceased, she called a family meeting to be held in behalf of said minors and composed of the nearest relatives of said minors for the purpose of deliberating touching the interest of said minors and more particularly to decide whether it was advisable and to the interest of said minors to sell at public auction the property belonging to the succession of said Etienne Aymond, deceased, and if so to fix the terms and conditions of the sale, which family meeting was held on the 3rd day of December A.D. 1870, the proceedings of which are herewith filed for reference. Wherefore she prays that an order of sale be granted and commission issue directed to Edward de Generes, public auctioneer authorizing and empowering him to sell at public auction after the legal delays and advertisements are had all the property and effects belonging to the said succession of Etienne Aymond, decd. On the terms and conditions recommended by said family meeting be homologated in all its parts and particulars.
And she prays for all other orders in the premises

A.H. Bordelon
Atty. For petitioner

Order

Let the proceedings of said family meeting be homologated in all its parts and particulars and let a commission issue directed to Edward de Generes, Esq. public auctioneer in and for the parish of Avoyelles authorizing and empowering him to sell at public auction after the legal delays and advertisements are had all the property and effects belonging to the succession of Etienne Aymond, deceased, on the terms and conditions recommended by said family meeting.
Parish Judge Office Marksville Avoyelles   December 7th A.D. 1870

J.M. Edwards
Parish Judge

Chapter 6: Marcellin Aymond and Ovelia Dupuy

Marcellin, called "Marcel" was born May 30, 1849 in Plaucheville. He was the second child of Etienne (Stephen) Aymond, II and Elodie Chenevert. Marcellin married Ovelia Dupuy (DOB: December 3, 1850) daughter of Theodore Alexis Dupuy and Zoe Scallan.

Marcellin Aymond and Ovelia Dupuy reared their family in the "Hickory" area near Plaucheville. Marcellin died in 1888 at the age of 39. His last child, Arthur, was born after Marcellin died. After his death, his wife Ovelia was left alone to rear five children. Her oldest son, O' Neil, helped her with his brothers and sisters, and worked to help support them.

Marcellin had been married for a brief time before he married Ovelia Dupuy. He married his first wife, Irma Firmin, on January 9, 1873. Their only child, a daughter, named Maria was born September 26, 1873. Maria Aymond married on November 21, 1889 to Ambroise David Saucier. Ordean and Carol Aymond, Sr. remember bringing Arthur (Maria's half-brother) and his wife, Emma, to visit Maria in Melville, La.

As Ovelia became older and her children were married, she spent time at each of their homes. She was living in Alexandria with her son, O'Neil and his wife Lucy, when she died in 1939. She is buried in Pineville.

Ordean Gaspard Aymond, wife of Carol J. Aymond, Sr., noted that when Carol was stationed in New Orleans and attending Delgado School for six months, she remembers walking to his Uncle Herman and Aunt Florida's (Marcellin's daughter) house to have supper. She remembers "fixing" Aunt Florida's hair when she went to visit. She said that Aunt Florida was a very proud lady and liked to look nice.

Another note from Ordean Gaspard Aymond was concerning her brother Dallas and his wife. She found it interesting that her brother at one time lived in the same house in Hickory as Marcellin and Ovelia.

Husband: Marcelin Aymond
DOB: May 30, 1849 - Plaucheville
Died: May 11, 1888
Buried: Mater Dolorosa Catholic Cemetery, Plaucheville, LA
Married: October 12, 1875, Church of the
Assumption, Avoyelles
Parents: Etienne Aymond (1816-1868)
        Elodie Chenevert (1824-1905)

Wife: Ovelia Dupuis
DOB: December 3, 1850
Died: October 17, 1939 or1937
Buried: Pineville, LA
Parents: Theodore Alexis
Dupuy (1815 -
Zoe Scallan (1814 -)

First Marriage to Irma or Irene Firmin on January 9, 1873 (Book C, p. 486).   They had one child, Marie, born in 1873.

Children of Marcellin and Ovelia

Name	DOB – DOD-Married	Married	Comments
O'Neil Aymond	DOB: 2/4/1878 M: 7/19/1899 DOD: 8/27/1943	Ura Glasscock DOB: 12/5/1878 Lucy Stewart	Marriage: Book G, Page 504 Ura's father was a steamboat captain from Kentucky
Leonce Aymond	DOB: 2/4/1880 M: 5/19/1907 DOD: 2/1/1961	Etna Ducote DOB:4/16/1886 DOD: 11/30/1964	Book H, p. 682
Victoria Aymond	DOB: 3/12/1882 Cottonport M: 11/7/1902 DOD: 8/19/1975 Port Neches, TX	Joseph Jeansonne	Book H, p. 176 She left Mr. Jeansonne when her children were young and lived in Fort Worth, TX with daughter, Ruth.
Florida Aymond	DOB: 1/1885 M: 1920	Herman Bordelon	
Arthur Aymond	DOB. 11/22/1887 M. 12/23/1915 DOD: 1/23/1962	Emma Louise Laborde DOB. 8/8/1888 Cottonport DOD. 5/15/1980 Cottonport	
Daughter of Marcelin Aymond and Irene Firmin			
Marie Louise Aymond	DOB: 9/26/1873 DOD: 3/23/1960 M: 11/21/1889	Ambroise D. Saucier	
Notes: Refer to Book C, Page 126 Courthouse records for marriage; Succession: Book C, p. 711, "Oaths & Bonds", June 2, 1888 Marriage Records: St. Paul's Catholic Church, Mansura, LA			

Certificate of Baptism

St. Paul the Apostle Church
MANSURA, LOUISIANA 71350

⇾ This is to Certify ⇽

That _Marcellin Aymond_

Child of _Etienne Aymond_

and _Elodie Chenevat_

born in _Avoyelles Parish, La_
(CITY)   (STATE)

on the _3d_ day of _May_ 19 _1849_

was

Baptized

on the _7_ day of _June_ 19 _1849_.

According to the Rite of the Roman Catholic Church

by the Rev. _M. T. Mazzuchelli_

the Sponsors being { _— Chauven_
                    Caroline Aymond

as appears from the Baptismal Register of this Church.

Dated _10-28/77_

Earl V. Provenza
Pastor

No. 314   F. J. REMEY CO., Inc.   MINEOLA, N.Y.

1850 Census

1850 United States Federal Census

Name:	**Marcel Louise**	
Age:	1	
Birth Year:	abt 1849	
Birthplace:	Louisiana	
Home in 1850:	Avoyelles, Louisiana	
Gender:	Male	
Family Number:	719	

Household Members:	Name	Age
	Etienne Aymond	34
	Elodie Aymond	23
	Marie Louise	5
	Marcel Louise	1

Source Citation: Year: *1850*; Census Place: *, Avoyelles, Louisiana*; Roll: *M432_229*; Page: *150A*; Image: *304*.

Source Information:

Ancestry.com. *1850 United States Federal Census* [database on-line]. Provo, UT, USA: Ancestry.com Operations, Inc., 2009. Images reproduced by FamilySearch.

Original data: Seventh Census of the United States, 1850; (National Archives Microfilm Publication M432, 1009 rolls); Records of the Bureau of the Census, Record Group 29; National Archives, Washington, D.C.

Description:
This database is an index to individuals enumerated in the 1850 United States Federal Census, the Seventh Census of the United States. Census takers recorded many details including each person's name, age as of the census day, sex, color; birthplace, occupation of males over age fifteen, and more. No relationships were shown between members of a household. Additionally, the names of those listed on the population schedule are linked to actual images of the 1850 Federal Census.

© 2013, The Generations Network, Inc.

81

 ancestry

1860 United States Federal Census

Name:	**Etienne Aymond**
Age in 1860:	44
Birth Year:	abt 1816
Birthplace:	Louisiana
Home in 1860:	Avoyelles, Louisiana
Gender:	Male
Post Office:	Marksville
Value of real estate:	

Household Members	Name	Age
	Etienne Aymond	44
	Elodie Aymond	36
	Marie Aymond	15
	Marcelin Aymond	10
	Virginie Aymond	8
	Irma Aymond	7
	Stephen Aymond	1

Source Citation: Year: *1860*; Census Place: , *Avoyelles, Louisiana*; Roll: *M653_407*; Page: *361*; Image: *361*; Family History Library Film: *803407*.

Source Information:

 THE NATIONAL ARCHIVES ARCHIVES.GOV

Ancestry.com. *1860 United States Federal Census* [database on-line]. Provo, UT, USA: Ancestry.com Operations, Inc., 2009. Images reproduced by FamilySearch.

Original data: 1860 U.S. census, population schedule. NARA microfilm publication M653, 1,438 rolls. Washington, D.C.: National Archives and Records Administration, n.d.

Description:
This database is an index to individuals enumerated in the 1860 United States Federal Census, the Eighth Census of the United States. Census takers recorded many details including each person's name, age as of the census day, sex, color; birthplace, occupation of males over age fifteen, and more. No relationships were shown between members of a household. Additionally, the names of those listed on the population schedule are linked to actual images of the 1860 Federal Census.

 ancestry

1870 United States Federal Census

Name:	**Marcel Aymond**
Age in 1870:	20
Birth Year:	abt 1850
Birthplace:	Louisiana
Home in 1870:	Subdivision 5, Avoyelles, Louisiana
Race:	White
Gender:	Male
Post Office:	Marksville
Value of real estate:	

Household Members:	Name	Age
	Irma Aymond	45
	Ferrier Aymond	21
	Irma Aymond	17
	Marcel Aymond	20
	Charles Johnson	23
	Louise Johnson	24
	Armas Juneau	7

Source Citation: Year: *1870*; Census Place: *Subdivision 5, Avoyelles,*
Louisiana; Roll: *M593_506*; Page: *475B*; Image: *326*; Family History Library Film: *552005*.

Source Information:

Ancestry.com. *1870 United States Federal Census* [database on-line]. Provo, UT, USA: Ancestry.com
Operations, Inc., 2009. Images reproduced by FamilySearch.

Original data:

- 1870 U.S. census, population schedules. NARA microfilm publication M593, 1,761 rolls. Washington, D.C.: National
  Archives and Records Administration, n.d.
- Minnesota census schedules for 1870. NARA microfilm publication T132, 13 rolls. Washington, D.C.: National
  Archives and Records Administration, n.d.

Description:
This database is an index to individuals enumerated in the 1870 United States Federal Census, the Ninth Census of the
United States. Census takers recorded many details including each person's name, age at last birthday, sex, color; birthplace,
occupation, and more. No relationships were shown between members of a household. Additionally, the names of those
listed on the population schedule are linked to actual images of the 1870 Federal Census.

Marriage of Marcelin and Irma Firmin
January 9, 1873
Although I couldn't find the original document, I located
this copy handwritten by my mother, Ordean G. Aymond

Marcelin Aymond and Irma Firmin 1-9-1873
Marriage Certificate

State of Louisiana }
Parish of Avoyelles } Be it known that on ninth day of
January AD — one thousand eight hundred and seventy
three before me, the undersigned in and for the parish
of Avoyelles personally came + appeared Marcelin
Aymond and wife Irma Firmin who has produced
the license required by law signify their intention and
desire to be united in the bonds of matrimony —
Whereupon, I the said _____ in presence
of the undersigned competents witnesses, did join the
said parties in wedlock and pronounce them man +
wife — and in faith whereof, the said parties, together
with the undersigned witness and me the said _____
have hereunto, on the day + year past aforesaid, signed
these presents —

C J Matthews   Marcelin X Aymond
D Chenevert   Irma + Firmin
C E Matthews   mark
                                 F E Simon Ptre

Book C, p. 486 in Marksville Courthouse

84

Marriage License of Marcellin
Aymond and Ovelia Dupuis
September 20, 1875

STATE OF LOUISIANA,

PARISH OF AVOYELLES.

To Rev. P. L. Simon, a Curate in and for

The Parish of Avoyelles, Greeting:

You are hereby licensed and permitted to unite in the bonds of Matrimony, according to law and established rules,

Mr. Marcellin Aymond

and Miss Ovelia Dupuis

And when you shall so have done, that you make duplicate acts of the celebration thereof, signed by yourself and three witnesses as required by law, one of which acts shall return within thirty days to the Office of the Clerk of the Seventh Judicial District Court, in and for the Parish of Avoyelles, together with this license.

Given under my hand and Seal of Office as Clerk of the District Court in and for the Parish of Avoyelles, the 20th day of September, eighteen hundred and seventy five.

R. B. Coco, Clerk.

Marriage Certificate
Marcellin Aymond and Ovelia Dupuis
October 12, 1875

STATE OF LOUISIANA,

Parish of Avoyelles.

Be it Known, that on this _Twelfth_ day of _October_ _A. D.,_ one thousand eight hundred and seventy-_five_ before me, the undersigned _____ in and for the parish of Avoyelles, personally came and appeared, Mr. _Marcellin Aymond_ and _Miss Ovilia Dupuis_ who having produced the license required by law, signify their intention and desire to be united in the bonds of matrimony.

Whereupon, I, the said _____ in the presence of the under-signed competent witnesses, did join the said parties in wedlock, and pronounce them man and wife.

In faith whereof, the said parties, together with the undersigned witnesses and me, the said _____ have hereunto, on the day, month and year past aforesaid, signed these presents.

Marcellin his + mark Aymond
Ovilia her + mark Dupuis

J. E. Aymond

WITNESSES:
Tamira Gravillon
Euphemin Gravillon
Eugée Gravillon

Marriage of Marcellin Aymond and
Olivia Dupuis
Filed November 15, 1875

Parish of Avoyelles

Be it known that on this twelfth day of October A.D. One thousand eight hundred and seventy-five before me, the undersigned in and for the parish of Avoyelles, personally came and appeared Mr. Marceline Aymond and Miss Olivia Dupuis who having produced the license required by law, Signify their intention and desire to be united in the bonds of Matrimony.

Whereupon, I the said   in the presence of the undersigned competent witnesses, do join the said parties in wedlock, and pronounce them man and wife.

In faith whereof the said parties together with the undersigned witnesses and me the said have hereinto, on the day, month and year aforesaid, signed these present:

Witnesses

S   Gremillion

Symphorien Couvillion

Eugee Gremillion

Marcelin X Aymond

Ovilia X Dupuis

T. E. Simon

Book D, page 90

Avoyelles Parish Court House

Marriage of Marcelin Aymond and Ovelia Dupuis
October 12, 1875

Parish of Avoyelles

Be it Known, that on this twelfth day of October A.D. One thousand eight hundred and Seventy-five before me, the undersigned in and for the parish of Avoyelles, personally came and appeared Mr Marcelin Aymond and Miss Olivia Dupuis who having produced the license required by law, Signify their intention and desire to be united in the bonds of Matrimony

Whereupon, I, the said ___ in the presence of the undersigned competent witnesses, did join the said parties in Wedlock, and pronounce them Man and Wife

In faith whereof, the said parties together with the undersigned witnesses and me, the said ___ have hereunto, on the day, month and year first aforesaid, Signed these presents.

Witnesses
Simeon Gremillion
Symphorien Gremillion
Eugée Gremillion

their
Marcelin X Aymond
Ovelia X Dupuis
marks

T. C. Simon
ph.

Margin notes:

MARCELIN Aymond
Olivia Dupuis
Marriage
Filed
15" Nov.
1875.

By: Ordean Gaspard
Aymond
Oct 27, 1977 —

My husband Carol
Aymond, Sr's grand
father & grand mother

Book D pg. 90

Marcelin Aymond son of
↑ Etienne Aymond
↓ Elodie Chenevert

Olivia Dupuis daughter
Theodore A Dupuis
2d "Score

Marcellin Aymond
was known as
"Marcel"

88

Zoe Scallan, widow Theodore Dupuy

Ovelia Dupuy wife of Marcelin Aymond

Sale of Land   Filed August 19, 1879

State of Louisiana

Parish of Avoyelles

        Be it known that on this 19th day of August in the year of our Lord One Thousand Eighteen and seventy-nine:

Before me Merile Lacour a   with regard for the Parish of Avoyelles, duly commissioned and qualified and in the presence of witnesses having the named and undersigned.

Personally came and appeared Zoe Scallan, widow of Theodore Dupuy a resident of the Parish of Avoyelles, State of Louisiana, consideration hereinafter mentioned she does by those present,

grant, bargained, sold, conveyed, transfer assign and deliver with full guarantee against all debt, mortgages, claims or other encumbrances whatsoever unto Ovelia Dupuy, wife of Marcelin Aymond, being duly aided, authorized and assisted by her husband of the Parish of Avoyelles State aforesaid, here present and purchasing for herself, her heir and assigns

and provisions thereof.

A certain tract of land containing eight and ¾ acres situated and   was Bayou Choupique , in the said Parish, bordered South by Fontaine Callagari ,by Mr. Keller, West by   Broussard and East by   with all the improvements.

This sale is made for and in consideration of the   and sum of one hundred and fifty dollars, cash in hand to the   will and truly paid the receipt is hereby   , and   in full therefore   to have   and to hold, the said property unto the said purchaser her heirs and assigned, to their proper   and   belief forever   the said   the said tract of land to the the heirs and assigns, shall and will   warrant   and   find against the lawful claims of all persons whatever by those present , and   the said   does   the said purchase of all the   and actions of warranty which he has   may have against her or against the   , fully authorizing the said purchaser to the said rights and actions in the same manner as her   might or could have done. The certificate of mortgage   by   3364 of the Civil Code of Louisiana,
on the subject of Lien and Mortgage   by the contracting parties who agree to free the undersigned   Notary Public from all responsibility for the   of the same. Thus done and issued at the residence of David Saucier with Emile Dupuy competent witness who hereto sign names as such,

after the reading thereof Zoe Scallan authorize my wife to sign.   Marcelin Aymond

      David Saucier   Emile Dupuy   Merile Lacour, Not. Pub.

89

Children (1)

Marie Aymond   B: 1873

Marcellin Aymond

B: 30 May 1849 in Avoyelles Parish, Louisiana
D: 11 May 1888 in Plaucheville, Avoyelles Parish, Louisiana

Parents

Etienne Aymond Jr.
1816-1868

Elodie Chenevert
1824-1905

Irma Firmin B: 9 Oct 1854 in
Avoyelles, Louisiana, United States

Other
spouses (1)

Marcellin Aymond
in the U.S., Find A Grave Index, 1600s-Current

✔ Saved to   Aymond, Marcellin in tree "Carol
Aymond family tree"   Remove

Suggested Records ❓

📄 U.S., Find A Grave Index,
1600s-Current
Marcelin Aymond

📄 Louisiana, Marriages,
1718-1925
Barcelin Aymond

📄 1880 United States
Federal Census
M. Aymond

📄 1880 United States
Federal Census
O. Aymond

Go to website

Want to get
involved? Click here!

⚠ Report issue

Name:	Marcellin Aymond
Birth Date:	7 Jun 1849
Birth Place:	Louisiana, USA
Death Place:	Louisiana, USA
Cemetery:	Saint Marys Assumption Catholic Cemetery
Burial or Cremation Place:	Cottonport, Avoyelles Parish, Louisiana, USA
Has Bio?:	Y
Spouse:	Ovelia Aymond
Children:	Arthur Joseph Aymond
URL:	http://www.findagrave.com/cgi-...

SAVE ⌄

Write a comment.

Make a Connection

Find others who are
researching Marcellin

Marcelin's grave is located in the Mater Dolorosa Catholic Cemetery, Plaucheville, LA

Succession of Marcelin Aymond deceased

Petition for Tutorship and Inventory

Filed May 18, 1888

To the Honorable the Judges of the 12th judicial District of Louisiana sitting in and for the Parish of Avoyelles. The petition of Mistress Ovelia Dupuis resident of your Partish respectfully shows that recently her husband Marcelin Aymond died in said Parish leaving a small estate of community property of their marriage. He also left minor children issue of their said marriage namely: Oneal, Leonce, Victoria, Florida, and Arthur Joseph Aymond. Petitioner desires to qualify as natural tutorix of her said minor children and in her capacity of tutorix administer upon the succession of her said deceased husband. It is also necessary that an under   tutor be appointed to said minors and ___ suggest the name Ferrier S. Aymond their paternal uncle as suitable person. Wherefore petitioner prays that a commission issue directed to ____ Lucerin notary Public in and for the Parish of Avoyelles authorizing and empowering him to take an estimative Inventory of the effects of the succession of Marcelin Aymond and to make due returns thereof to your Honorable _____

Petitioner ___ to be permitted to qualify ….. (the remainder of this page was missing)

Book C, Page 711

Succession of Marcelin Aymond

May 18, 1888

May 18, 1888 Marcelin Aymond (died) (1)

Thomas Overton Judge 12th Judl Dist

Succession of Marcelin Aymond deceased
Petition for Tutorship and Inventory
Filed May 15th 1888

To the Honorable the Judges of the 12th Judicial District of Louisiana sitting in and for the Parish of Avoyelles.

The petition of Mistress Ombia Dupuis resident of your Parish respectfully shows that recently her husband Marcelin Aymond died in said Parish leaving a small estate of community property of their marriage, he also left minor children issue of their said marriage namely; Omeal Louise Victoria Florida and Arthur Joseph Aymond. Petitioner desires to qualify as natural tutrix of her said minor children and also in her capacity of tutrix administer upon the succession of her said deceased husband. It is also necessary that an undertutor be appointed to said minors and petitioner suggest the name Ferrier Aymond their paternal uncle as a suitable person.

Wherefore petitioner prays that a commission issue directed to Mr. Lacour notary Public in and for the Parish of Avoyelles authorizing and empowering him to take an estimative Inventory of the effects of the succession of Marcelin Aymond and to make due returns thereof to your honorable Court [illegible] that she be permitted to qualify

> Order for Succession
> May 18, 1888

The foregoing duly considered it is ordered that a commission issue a _____ to M___ Lacour notary Public in and for the Parish of Avoyelles authorizing him to take a true and estimative Inventory of the effects of the succession of Marcelin Aymond deceased and to make due returns thereof to this Court Let petitioner qualify as natural tutrix of her said minor children and in her capacity of tutrix let her administer upon said estate. Let Ferrier S. Aymond qualify as under tutor of said minors

Granted in chambers on this 18ᵗʰ day of May… (the remainder of the page was missing)

Ovelia Dupuy Aymond
Dec. 12, 1850-
Oct. 17, 1939

I was told by my father, Carol Aymond, Sr., that his grandmother, Ovelia, was tall. She liked to sit on the front porch of the big house where they lived on Bayou LaBlue in Hickory. His father, Arthur, their son, used to hunt around the little lake nearby. After Marcellin died, she lived part time at the homes of her sons; O'Neil in Alexandria, Arthur and Emma, or with Leonce at his home on Indian Bayou. She lived during the Civil War (ll-13 yrs old). She said that she remembered the Indians.

Oneal Aymond, Florida Aymond, Arthur Aymond,

Victoria Aymond and Leonce Aymond

Marcelin Aymond died on May 11, 1888, at the young age of thirty-nine. He is buried in the
Mater Dolorosa Catholic Cemetery located in Plaucheville, Louisiana.
This headstone was placed by Marcelin's grandson,
Carol J. Aymond, Sr. who often visited the grave of his grandfather.

Chapter 7: Arthur Aymond and Emma Louise Laborde

Arthur Joseph Aymond was born on November of 1887 and grew up in Hickory, near Plaucheville. His parents were Marcellin Aymond and Ovelia Dupuy Aymond. Arthur never knew his father, Marcellin, as he died at the age of 39 before Arthur was born. O'Neil, the oldest child of Marcellin ad Ovelia, worked in the field and helped his mother to rear his four brothers and sisters after the death of his father.

Emma Louise Laborde was born in Avoyelles Parish and was reared in Indian Bayou with her five brothers and sisters; Charles, Winnie, Bennett, Arthur, and Ludger. Her parents were Alphonse Laborde and Louise Gauthier Laborde. Her family's home was located on the 58 acres that she and Arthur would later buy and farm. Emma and Arthur were married on December 23, 1915 in Cottonport. Arthur was 28 years old and Emma was 27. They had four children; Odel, Herman, Carol, and Burton.

Arthur's first job was with the railroad where he worked as an engineer and brakeman. An accident occurred when he was opening a boxcar connector, which closed on his hand, crushing it. Later he worked as an overseer for a sugarcane plantation in Melville. The sugarcane was then shipped by rail to Cottonport and sent to the sugar mill in Dora Bend, between Cottonport and Evergreen (Highway 1184), for processing. The remains of that sugar mill can still be seen on the Dora Bend Road. The plantation furnished a horse for him to ride the plantation and oversee at least 300 men cutting cane by hand.

Later, Arthur returned to Cottonport to farm. He bought the Laborde property in Indian Bayou from his wife's family and began farming. It was on this same property that he and Emma built their home, using materials from the old Laborde home to build their home. Arthur planted cotton, corn and beans. He farmed with two mules (Bob and George) and a plow to cultivate his crop. These mules were wild when he got them. They came from Texas, Oklahoma, or Missouri in boxcars and brought here to sell to farmers. His son, Carol, remembers a particular incident with the mules. These mules knew exactly what to do in the field, walk next to the cotton and turn automatically on the ends of the rows. When the dinner bell rang at 11:30 each day, they knew exactly what that meant, rest and water.

Once George, the mule, had a bad accident. A mowing machine was parked under the barn. George got into a fight with a horse under the barn and jumped between the horse and mower blades. He was skinned for an area of about 2 sq. feet. Arthur stitched him up the best he could and cared for George, but George wasn't getting any better. Arthur decided to turn him loose in the pasture and fully expected him to die. To their surprise, George began to get better and made a full recovery.

Emma's parents large Laborde home was eventually torn down and the lumber was used to build a home for Arthur and Emma. Arthur and Emma moved into their "new" home on May 27, 1932. Many years later, when Carol Aymond tore down his parents' home, the wood was used to build cypress benches for each of his children in memory of their grandparents. The old home site is the present location of the Aymond Cemetery on Indian Bayou Road in Cottonport (shown right).

I won second place, for hat

Emma was a loving mother and grandmother. She loved to cook and sew. She often entered her baking in local festivals. She had many blue ribbons for winning those competitions. She once won a $50.00 U.S. Savings bond and a gold ribbon at the Louisiana Livestock and Pasture Festival held in Marksville. Her Sweetheart Coffee Bread was judged the best. She also took home two blue ribbons that day for her entry of Holiday Bread.

A large write-up appeared in the Alexandria Daily Town Talk, which included her recipe for her Sweetheart Bread. On the previous page is a photo in which she won second place for the hat which she entered in a "Hat Contest".

Emma also loved to have sleepovers with her granddaughters. It was not unusual for her to decide at 10:00 p.m. to make a cake or some other kind of sweet. One particular cake I recall which was one of her favorites was an apple cake. She also made the best homemade chocolate syrup for ice-cream sundaes. Spending time with her on those special nights created memories that I'll always treasure.

I can still remember the nights going to sleep at my grandparents' house. They often had some of their friends over to play "Booray", a well-known card game. They sat in the dining area at their round oak dining table, laughing and joking with their friends. She always provided one of her delicious deserts for them to enjoy, which they shared with me.

Emma also loved gardening. We spent many afternoons walking in the yard and checking on the status of her outdoor flowers. As we walked around, she would tell me the names of each flower. I remember her having a Hydrangea plant on the right side of the house which made beautiful blue flowers. To this day, I have a special fondness for this plant because of the memories of spending time with my grandmother.

I remember my grandfather, Arthur, as a mild-mannered man. I can never remember him ever raising his voice. My grandmother would send him to school in their car, to pick me up in the afternoon when I was going to sleep at their house. They lived near school, but she did not want me walking on the road. Because I always had to ride the bus to come and go from my own home, I always wanted to be able to walk home like the "town" kids. So, I sometimes acted like I didn't see him waiting for me and hurriedly took off down the road to walk back. He never scolded me for this, even though I'm sure he knew that I had done it purposely.

Arthur continued to farm and raise cattle. He was a heavy smoker all his adult life and later developed pancreatic cancer. He died on January 23, 1962. Emma live to be ninety-one years old. She died of cardiac arrest on May 15, 1980. I often think of them; they have a very special place in my heart.

Husband: **Arthur Joseph Aymond**
DOB: November 22, 1887 Plaucheville, LA
Died: January 23, 1962
Buried: Aymond Cemetery, Cottonport, LA

Married: December 23, 1915 in Cottonport, LA
Occupation: Farmer and Railroad Engineer
Parents: Marcellin Aymond (1849-1888)
Ovelia Dupuy (1850-1939)

Wife: **Emma Louise Laborde**
DOB: August 8, 1888
Died: May 15, 1980
Buried: Aymond Cemetery
Cottonport, LA
Parents: Alphonse Laborde
Louise Gauthier

Children:

Name	DOB - DOD	Married	Comments
Odel Katherine	DOB: 10/22/1916 M: DOD: Bapt. 11/14/1916	Ernest "Fuzzy" Hanchey From El Paso, Texas	They lived in Baton Rouge, LA. Odel was a registered nurse and a dietitian at LSU. She is buried in Cottonport in the Aymond Cemetery on Indian Bayou Road.
Herman Anthony	DOB: 5/17/1918 M: DOD: 10/13/1991 Bapt: 6/18/1918	Pauline Pratt from Georgia, they met while he was in service in Columbus, Georgia. Herman adopted her son, Billy. They later adopted Vickie.	Herman was a cotton farmer then later sold the property to his brother Carol. He then was a trucker who hauled dirt, gravel, and asphalt. He also raised cattle. He is buried in Cottonport, LA.
Carol James	DOB: 7/14/1921 M:7/26/2942 DOD:12/18/2016	Ordean Marie Gaspard	They lived in Cottonport, on Dora Bend Road (Hwy 1184). Ordean was a homemaker and stay-at-home mother for her five children.
Burton Joseph	DOB: 4/23/1932 M: DOD:	Helena Dauzat from the Effie area. She married Burton after her first husband died. She met Burton in the cemetery in Cottonport.	Burton worked at Avondale Shipyard in New Orleans as a welder/fitter. He and his wife lived in Kenner, LA. They had two sons, Kirk and Burton, Jr.
Notes:			

ST. MARY'S ASSUMPTION CHURCH

COTTONPORT, LOUISIANA

⤙ This is to Certify ⤚

That _Emma Labade_

Child of _Alphonse Labade_

and _Louise Gauthier_

born in _Cottonport_ , _La_
(CITY) (STATE)

on the _8th_ day of _August_ 1888

was **Baptized**

on the _5th_ day of _July_ 1889

According to the Rite of the Roman Catholic Church

by the Rev. _G. Rechatin_

the Sponsors being { _Nestor Gauthier_ _Flavie Juno_

as appears from the Baptismal Register of this Church.

Dated _3/15/78_

Msgr. Russel J. Ritchie

Pastor

```
┌─────────────────────────────────┐
│       Marriage License of       │
│        Arthur and Emma          │
│       December 18, 1915         │
└─────────────────────────────────┘
```

Arthur Aymond & Emma Laborde

STATE OF LOUISIANA,

Parish of *Avoyelles*   Know All Men by These Presents :

THAT WE, *Arthur Aymond* .... as Principal, and

.... *Alphonse Laborde* .... as Security, acknowledge
to owe to the Governor of the State of Louisiana, or his successor or successors in office, the sum of ONE HUNDRED DOLLARS, the payment of
which we hereby bind ourselves, our heirs and administrators, in solido.

Given under our hands at *Marksville, La.*, this *18th* day of *December*, A. D. 191*5*

The Condition of the Above Obligation Is Such,

That, whereas, the above bounden *Arthur Aymond*

has this day obtained a license from the Clerk of the District Court of the Parish of *Avoyelles* .... to marry with

Emma Laborde

Now, if at the time said license was granted, there existed no legal impediments or obstacle to the celebration of said marriage, then, and in
such case, this obligation to be null and void; otherwise to remain in full force and virtue in law.

Arthur Laborde

Alphonse his Laborde
mk.

Name of Man *Arthur Aymond*	Name of Woman *Emma Laborde*
Age *27* Residence	Age *22* Residence
Mother *Ovelia Dupuis*	Mother
Residence	Residence
Father *Marcelin Aymond*	Father
Residence	Residence
Former Wife ⎰ Dead ⎱ Living	Former Husband ⎰ Dead ⎱ Living

Relationship of contracting parties ....

101

 ancestry·

Children (4)

Odell Aymond Hanchey	B: 1916
Herman A. AYMOND	B: 1918
Carol James	B: 1921

 Arthur Aymond

B: Nov 22, 1887 in Hickory Hill, Marksville, Avoyelles Parish, Louisiana
D: 23 Jan 1962 in Bunkie, Avoyelles Parish, Louisiana

Parents

Marcellin Aymond
1849-1888

Felicite Ovelia DUPUIS
1849-1939

Emma Laborde B: 08 Aug 1888 in Cottonport, Avoyelles Parish, Louisiana

Arthur Aymond
in the U.S., WWI Civilian Draft Registrations, 1917-1918

✓ Saved to Aymond, Arthur in tree "Carol Aymond family tree"   Remove

Index-only record

🖉 Add alternate information

⚠ Report issue

Name:	Aymond, Arthur
Birth Date:	22 Nov 1887
Birth Place:	Cottonport LA
City/County:	Avoyelles
State:	LA
Ethnicity:	W

SAVE ⌄

Source Information
Ancestry.com. *U.S., WWI Civilian Draft Registrations, 1917-1918* [database on-line]. Provo, UT, USA: Ancestry.com Operations Inc, 2000.

Original data: Banks, Ray, comp.. *World War I Civilian Draft Registrations*.

Description
This database provides information on 1.2 million men in the United States born between 1873 and 1900 who completed draft registration cards in 1917 and 1918. Information found on these cards generally

Suggested Records ❓

📄 U.S., Social Security Applications and Claims Index, 1936-2007
Arthur J Aymond

📄 U.S., World War II Draft Registration Cards, 1942
Arthur Joseph Aymond

📄 1920 United States Federal Census
Arthur Aymond

📄 1910 United States Federal Census
Arthur Aymond

📄 1910 United States Federal Census
Arthur Van Aymond

📄 1940 United States Federal Census
Arthur Aymond

Show More ⌄

102

U.S., World War I Draft Registration Cards, 1917-1918 record for Arthur Aymond

Record Index

Name: Arthur Aymond

Source Information

103

 ancestry

1920 United States Federal Census

Name:	**Arthur Aynond** **[Arthur Aymond]**
Age:	32
Birth Year:	abt 1888
Birthplace:	Louisiana
Home in 1920:	Police Jury Ward 9, Avoyelles, Louisiana
Race:	White
Gender:	Male
Relation to Head of House:	Head
Marital Status:	Married
Spouse's Name:	Emma Aynond
Father's Birthplace:	Louisiana
Mother's Birthplace:	Louisiana
Home owned:	Rent
Able to read:	Yes
Able to Write:	Yes
Neighbors:	

Household Members:	Name	Age
	Arthur Aynond	32
	Emma Aynond	30
	Odel Aynond	3
	Herman Aynond	2

Source Citation: Year: *1920*; Census Place: *Police Jury Ward 9, Avoyelles, Louisiana*; Roll: *T625_605*; Page: *3B*; Enumeration District: *14*; Image: *588*.

Emma's Poll Book Registration Certif.

August 21, 1939

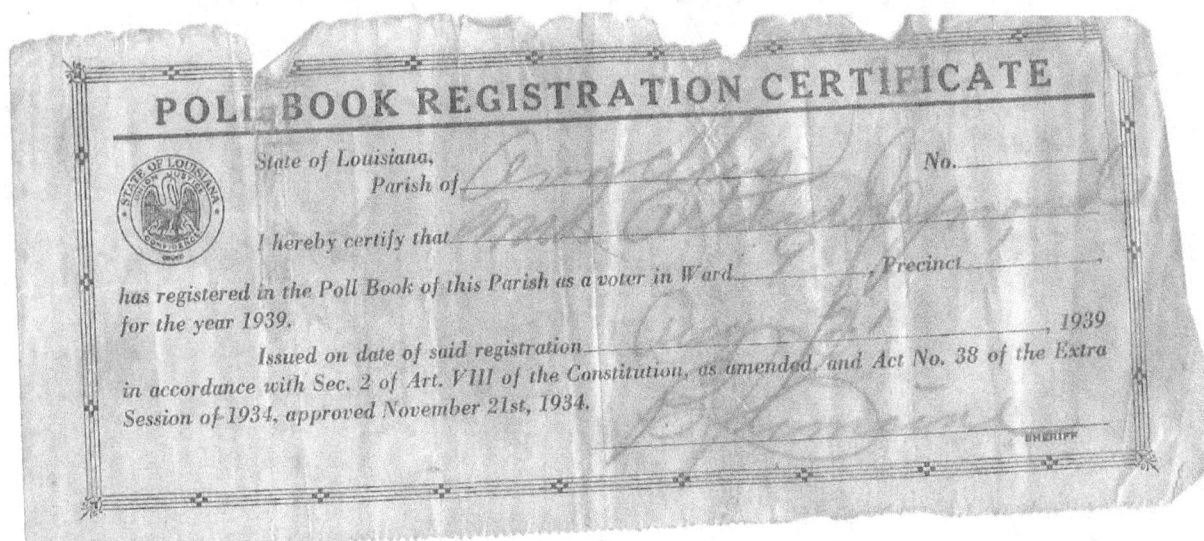

105

ancestry

1940 United States Federal Census

Name:	**Arthur J Aymond**
Respondent:	Yes
Age:	51
Estimated Birth Year:	abt 1889
Gender:	Male
Race:	White
Birthplace:	Louisiana
Marital Status:	Married
Relation to Head of House:	Head
Home in 1940:	Cottonport, Avoyelles, Louisiana
Farm:	Yes
Inferred Residence in 1935:	Cottonport, Avoyelles, Louisiana
Residence in 1935:	Same House
Sheet Number:	12B
Number of Household in Order of Visitation:	232
Occupation:	Farmer
House Owned or Rented:	Owned
Value of Home or Monthly Rental if Rented:	2000
Attended School or College:	No
Highest Grade Completed:	Elementary school, 5th grade
Hours Worked Week Prior to Census:	20
Class of Worker:	Working on own account
Weeks Worked in 1939:	52
Income:	0

106

Income Other Sources: Yes

Neighbors:

Household Members:

Name	Age
Arthur J Aymond	51
Emma Aymond	48
Herman Aymond	21
Carol Aymond	18
Burton Aymond	7

Source Citation: Year: *1940*; Census Place: *Cottonport, Avoyelles, Louisiana*; Roll: *T627_1382*; Page: *12B*; Enumeration District: *5-23*.

Source Information:
Ancestry.com. *1940 United States Federal Census* [database on-line]. Provo, UT, USA: Ancestry.com Operations, Inc., 2012. Original data: United States of America, Bureau of the Census. *Sixteenth Census of the United States, 1940*. Washington, D.C.: National Archives and Records Administration, 1940. T627, 4,643 rolls.

Description:
The 1940 United States Federal Census is the largest census released to date and the most recent census available for public access. The census gives us a glimpse into the lives of Americans in 1940, with details about a household's occupants that include birthplaces, occupations, education, citizenship, and income.

107

U.S., World War I Draft Registration Cards, 1917-1918 record for Arthur Aymond

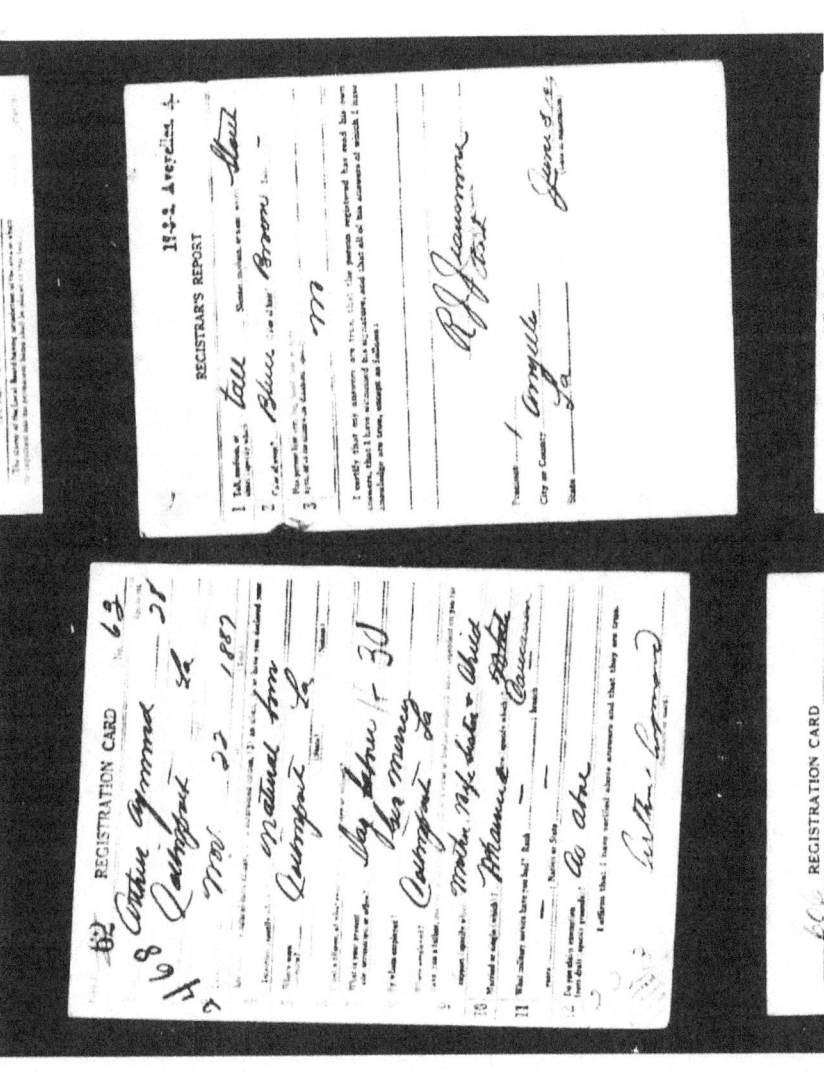

108

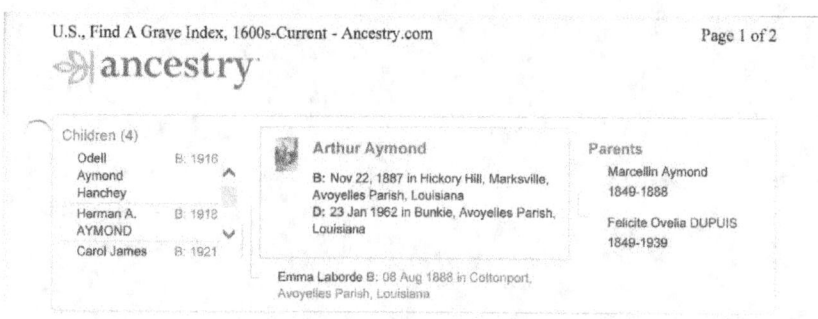

Children (4)

Odell Aymond Hanchey	B: 1916
Herman A. AYMOND	B: 1918
Carol James	B: 1921

Arthur Aymond

B: Nov 22, 1887 in Hickory Hill, Marksville, Avoyelles Parish, Louisiana

D: 23 Jan 1962 in Bunkie, Avoyelles Parish, Louisiana

Parents

Marcellin Aymond
1849-1888

Felicite Ovelia DUPUIS
1849-1939

Emma Laborde B: 08 Aug 1888 in Cottonport, Avoyelles Parish, Louisiana

Arthur Joseph Aymond
in the U.S., Find A Grave Index, 1600s-Current

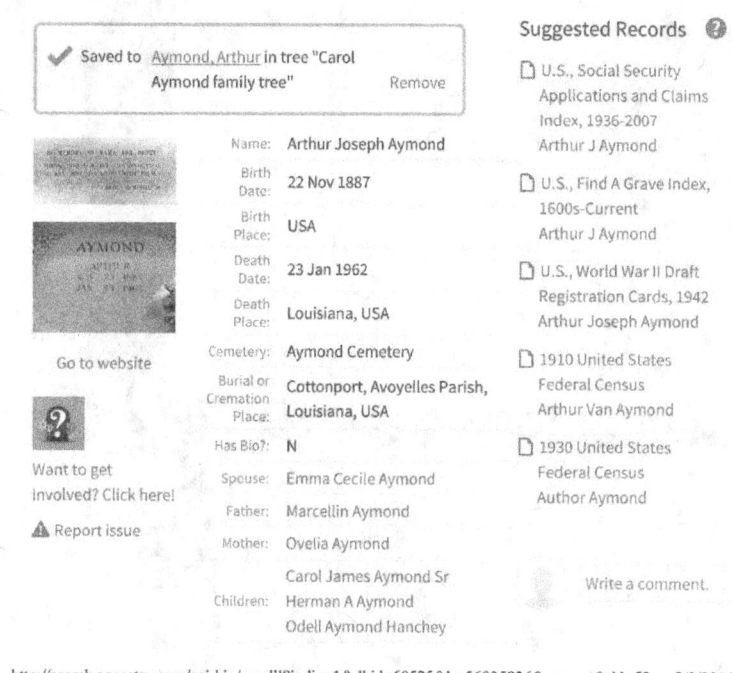

✔ Saved to Aymond, Arthur in tree "Carol Aymond family tree"   Remove

Go to website

Want to get involved? Click here!

⚠ Report issue

Name:	Arthur Joseph Aymond
Birth Date:	22 Nov 1887
Birth Place:	USA
Death Date:	23 Jan 1962
Death Place:	Louisiana, USA
Cemetery:	Aymond Cemetery
Burial or Cremation Place:	Cottonport, Avoyelles Parish, Louisiana, USA
Has Bio?:	N
Spouse:	Emma Cecile Aymond
Father:	Marcellin Aymond
Mother:	Ovelia Aymond
Children:	Carol James Aymond Sr Herman A Aymond Odell Aymond Hanchey

Suggested Records ❓

📄 U.S., Social Security Applications and Claims Index, 1936-2007
Arthur J Aymond

📄 U.S., Find A Grave Index, 1600s-Current
Arthur J Aymond

📄 U.S., World War II Draft Registration Cards, 1942
Arthur Joseph Aymond

📄 1910 United States Federal Census
Arthur Van Aymond

📄 1930 United States Federal Census
Author Aymond

Write a comment.

109

BIRTH No._____

STATE OF LOUISIANA

CERTIFICATE OF DEATH

STATE FILE No. 0 110

PERSONAL DATA OF DECEASED (Type or print names. Do not use numerals for month of death.)	1a. Last Name of Deceased *Aymond*	1b. First Name *Arthur*	1c. Second Name *J.*	2a. Month Day Year Date Of Death: *Jan 23-62*	2b. Hour *18?* M.

3. Sex — Male or Female *Male* | 4. Color or Race *White* | 5. Married ☒ Never Married ☐ Widowed ☐ Divorced ☐ | 6a. Name of Husband or Wife *Emma Labere* | 6b. Age *72*

7. Date of Birth of Deceased *Nov 22-1886* | 8. Age of Deceased: Years *75* Months Days | If under 24 Hrs. Hours Min. | 9a. Birthplace (City and State) *Cottonport, La* | 9b. Citizen of what Country *U.S.A.*

10a. Usual Occupation (Give kind of work done during most of working life, even if retired) *Farmer* | 10b. Kind of Industry or Business *Farming* | 11. Was Deceased ever in U. S. Armed Forces? (Yes, no, or unknown) *no* | 11a. Was Deceased ever... *no* | 11a. Social Security No.

PLACE OF DEATH	12a. City, Town, or Location *Bunkie*	12b. Parish *Avoyelles*	12c. Length of Stay in this Place *1 week*

12d. Name of Hospital or Institution (If not in hospital or institution give street address or location) *Temple Infirmary* | 12e. Is Place of Death inside City Limits? Yes ☒ No ☐

USUAL RESIDENCE OF DECEASED (Where deceased lived. If institution: Residence before admission)	13. City or Town *Cottonport*	13b. Parish *Avoyelles*	13c. State *La*

13d. Street Address—(If rural give location) *RFD* | 13e. Is Residence inside City Limits? Yes ☐ No ☒ | 13f. Is Residence on a Farm? Yes ☒ No ☐

PARENTS	14a. Name of Father *Marcelle Aymond*	14b. Birthplace of Father (City or town) *Plancheville, La*	15a. Maiden Name of Mother *Mary Dupuis*	15b. Birthplace of Mother (City or town) *Plancheville, La*

INFORMANT'S CERTIFICATION	I certify that the above stated information is true and correct to the best of my knowledge.	16a. Signature of Informant	16b. Date of Signature *Jan. 23-62*

CAUSE OF DEATH Enter only one cause per line for (a), (b) and (c)	17. Part I. Death was caused by: Immediate cause (a) *Coronary Occlusion*		Interval Between Onset and Death *3 days*

Conditions, if any, which gave rise to above cause (a), stating the underlying cause last. Due to (b) _____ Due to (c) _____

Part II. Other Significant conditions contributing to death but not related to the Terminal Disease condition given in Part I (a) | 18. Autopsy Yes ☐ No ☐

DEATHS DUE TO EXTERNAL VIOLENCE	19a. Accident ☐ Suicide ☐ Homicide ☐	19b. Describe how Injury Occurred. (Enter nature of injury in Part I or Part II of item 17.)

19c. Time Of Injury Hour a. m. p. m. Month, Day, Year | 19d. Injury Occurred While at Work ☐ Not While At Work ☐ | 19e. Place of Injury (e. g., in or about home, farm, factory, street, office bldg., etc.) | 19f. City, Town, or Location Parish State

PHYSICIAN'S CERTIFICATION	20. I certify that I attended the deceased From *1-19-62* To *1-23-62* and that death occurred on the date and hour stated above.	21a. Signature of Physician	21b. Date of Signature *1/24/62*

FUNERAL DIRECTOR'S CERTIFICATION	22a. Burial.... ☒ Cremation . ☐ Removal .. ☐ Date Thereof *Jan. 25-62*	22b. Name and Location of Cemetery or Crematory *Catholic Cemetery, Cottonport, La*	23. Signature and Address of Funeral Director *Joseph Amelle, Bunkie*

BURIAL TRANSIT PERMIT	24. Burial Transit Permit Number *05-2469A*	25. Parish of Issue *Avoyelles*	26. Date of Issue *1/25/62*	27. Signature of Local Registrar *Kendrick Taylor M.D. M.P.H.*

Certificate of Death for
Emma Laborde Aymond
May 17, 1980

IMPORTANT:
Black Ink or Typewriter
Ribbon Mandatory
By State Law.

BIRTH
NO.

STATE OF LOUISIANA
CERTIFICATE OF DEATH

STATE FILE NO. **119**

1A. LAST NAME OF DECEASED	1B. FIRST NAME	1C. SECOND NAME	2A. MONTH DAY YEAR		2B. HOUR

PERSONAL DATA OF DECEASED

(Type or print names. Do not use numerals for month of death.)

1A. **AYMOND** — 1B. **EMMA** — 1C. **LABORDE** — 2A. DATE OF DEATH **MAY 15 1980** — 2B. HOUR **6:00 P.M**

3. SEX—MALE OR FEMALE **FEMALE** — 4. COLOR OR RACE **WHITE** — 5. Married ☐ Never Married ☐ Widowed ☒ Divorced ☐ — 6. NAME OF HUSBAND OR WIFE **ARTHUR AYMOND , DEC.**

7. DATE OF BIRTH OF DECEASED **AUGUST 8 1888** — 8. AGE OF DECEASED YEARS **91** MONTHS DAYS HOURS MIN — 9A. BIRTHPLACE (CITY AND STATE) **COTTONPORT, LA.** — 9B. CITIZEN OF WHAT COUNTRY **U. S. A.**

10A. USUAL OCCUPATION (GIVE KIND OF WORK DONE DURING MOST OF WORKING LIFE, EVEN IF RETIRED) **HOUSEWIFE** — 10B. KIND OF BUSINESS OR INDUSTRY **DOMESTIC** — 11. SOCIAL SECURITY NUMBER **439 76 2213**

PLACE OF DEATH

12A. CITY, TOWN, OR LOCATION OF DEATH **MANSURA** — 12B. PARISH OF DEATH **AVOYELLES**

12C. NAME OF HOSPITAL OR INSTITUTION (IF NOT IN HOSPITAL OR INSTITUTION GIVE STREET ADDRESS OR LOCATION) **RIO SOL NURSING HOME** — 12D. IS PLACE OF DEATH INSIDE CITY LIMITS? Yes ☒ No ☐

USUAL RESIDENCE OF DECEASED

(Where deceased lived. If institution: Residence before admission.)

13A. CITY OR TOWN **COTTONPORT** — 13B. PARISH **AVOYELLES** — 13C. STATE **LOUISIANA**

13D. STREET ADDRESS—IF RURAL GIVE LOCATION **RFD RT. 1 INDIAN BAYOU ROAD** — 13E. IS RESIDENCE INSIDE CITY LIMITS? Yes ☒ No ☐

PARENTS

14. FATHER'S NAME — LAST **LABORDE** FIRST **ALPHONSE** MIDDLE — 15. MOTHER'S MAIDEN NAME — LAST **GAUTHIER** FIRST **LOUISE** MIDDLE

INFORMANT'S CERTIFICATION

I certify that the above stated information is true and correct to the best of my knowledge. — 16A. SIGNATURE OF INFORMANT *Carol Aymond Jr.* RT B Box 282 Cottonport, La. 71327 — 16B. DATE OF SIGNATURE **MAY 16 1980**

CAUSE OF DEATH

PART I. DEATH WAS CAUSED BY — ENTER ONLY ONE CAUSE PER LINE FOR (A), (B) AND (C)

17. IMMEDIATE CAUSE

Conditions, if any, which gave rise to immediate cause (a), stating the underlying cause last.

(a) *Cardiac Arrest* — DUE TO OR AS A CONSEQUENCE OF — INTERVAL BETWEEN ONSET AND DEATH

(b) *Congestive Heart Failure* — DUE TO OR AS A CONSEQUENCE OF

(c) *Atherosclerosis*

PART II. OTHER SIGNIFICANT CONDITIONS CONDITIONS CONTRIBUTING TO DEATH BUT NOT RELATED TO CAUSE GIVEN IN PART I (A) — 18A. AUTOPSY? Yes ☐ No ☐ — 18B. IF YES WERE FINDINGS CONSIDERED IN DETERMINING CAUSE OF DEATH? Yes ☐ No ☐

DEATH DUE TO EXTERNAL VIOLENCE

19A. ACCIDENT ☐ SUICIDE ☐ HOMICIDE ☐ — 19B. DESCRIBE HOW INJURY OCCURRED (ENTER NATURE OF INJURY IN PART I OR PART II OF ITEM 17.)

19C. TIME OF INJURY HOUR MONTH DAY YEAR ___ M.

19D. INJURY OCCURRED WHILE AT WORK ☐ NOT WHILE AT WORK ☐ — 19E. PLACE OF INJURY AT HOME, FARM, STREET, FACTORY, OFFICE BLDG, ETC (SPECIFY) — 19F. CITY, TOWN, OR LOCATION **COTTONPORT, LA. 71327** PARISH STATE

PHYSICIAN'S CERTIFICATION

20. I CERTIFY THAT I ATTENDED THE DECEASED From **1/25/80** To **Death** and that death occurred on the date and hour stated above. — 21A. SIGNATURE OF PHYSICIAN *J. M. Jackson M.D.* — 21B. DATE OF SIGNATURE *May 16, 1980*

FUNERAL DIRECTOR'S CERTIFICATION

22A. Burial ☒ Cremation ☐ Removal ☐ DATE THEREOF **May 17 1980** — 22B. NAME AND LOCATION OF CEMETERY OR CREMATORY **ST. MARYS Assumption Cem. Cottonport La.** — 23. SIGNATURE AND ADDRESS OF FUNERAL *ESCUDE F. H. COTTONPORT 412*

BURIAL TRANSIT PERMIT

24. BURIAL TRANSIT PERMIT NUMBER — 25. PARISH OF ISSUE **AVOYELLES** — 26. DATE OF ISSUE **MAY 16 1980** — 27. SIGNATURE OF LOCAL REGISTRAR

1S 16 — DHHR, OFFICE OF HEALTH SERVICES AND ENVIRONMENTAL QUALITY, VITAL RECORDS REGISTRY

Emma on the steps of her home

Arthur & Emma holding
grandchildren, Eddie and Ernest,

with Burton

Arthur Aymond, second from the left when he worked for the railroad

Home of Emma Laborde Aymond on Indian Bayou Road in Cottonport. Emma is on the far right.

113

--

Emma and her sister, Winnie

Herman on the cow, Carol kneeling, Geraldine (Gerry) Gauthier?, Odel?

Herman, Odel, and Carol Aymond

Home of Arthur and Emma Laborde Aymond located on Indian Bayou Road. It was built with lumber taken from the Laborde home.

Odel Aymond Hanchey

Emma and Odel at Odel's house in Baton Rouge

HANCHEY, ODELL AYMOND
A retired registered nurse and a resident of Baton Rouge, she died Friday, June 15, 2001, at Landmark Nursing Home in Baton Rouge. She was 84 and a native of Cottonport. Memorial Mass at Our Lady of Mercy Catholic Church, 445 Marquette Ave., at 2 p.m. Monday, celebrated by the Rev. Mike Moroney. Survived by two sons, Ernest and Eddie Hanchey, both of Dallas; two brothers, Carol Aymond of Cottonport and Burton Aymond of New Orleans; five grandchildren, Christopher Hanchey, Lee Anderson, John Hanchey, Dana Caddell and Cady Sunsdahl; and three great-grandchildren, Nick Deishler, Madison Sunsdahl and Arlee Caddell. In lieu of flowers, the family requests memorial donations be made to Our Lady of Mercy Catholic Church, 445 Marquette Ave., Baton Rouge, LA 70806.

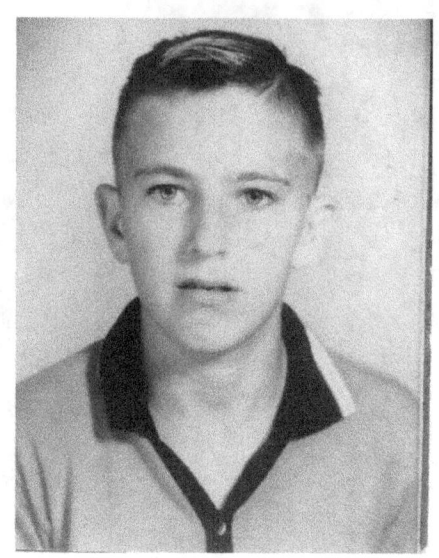

WWI picture of Emma's brother Charles Laborde.
Note the strong resemblance to his great-nephew,
Carol Aymond, Jr. on the right

Ovelia Dupuy Aymond
Dec. 12, 1850 –
Oct. 17, 1939

Emma's parents: Alphonse and Louise
Gauthier Laborde and two of their
children, Charles on the left and Bennett
on the right. Emma had cut out her
picture because she didn't like it.

117

Letter written by Odel to her mother, Emma

Dearest Mamma,

I hope you made it home O.K. Sorry that I wasn't there to meet you. Well I had a fine trip to Oklahoma & having a wonderful time.

Well I have been elected President of the Association — Southwestern College Health Association. Arkansas, Texas, Louisiana, Oklahoma & New Mexico. I am quiet proud of this as it is quiet an honor.

About the dog, the people went to Cottonport Saturday & got the dog. They were very upset about what happened & called me when they got home to let me know that they did have the dog and they were very upset because the dog had been beaten. This fellow that you gave the dog to had sold another dog acting as though it was the one that you had given him he had put his collar on another dog.

Well I will have to close as I have to go — will write more later — Take care of yourself.

YOUR CAMPUS HOTEL Love Odell

118

STOOL CLINIC AT AVOYELLES TRADE SCHOOL

The Home Demonstration Club members of Cottonport, Mansura and Indian Bayou attended a Stool Clinic at the Avoyelles Parish Trade School. Thirty-one ladies attended the clinic under the direction of Mr. Douglas A. Ducote, School Instructor, and Miss Edna Mae Morris, Home Demonstration Agent.

The stools made at the Trade School were woven on Wednesday, July 16th, in Cottonport, at the home of Mrs. Curley Poret; Thursday, July 17th, in Mansura, at the home of Mrs. George A. Chatelain; and Friday, July 18th, in Indian Bayou, at the home of Mrs. Alton Ducote.

Shown above are nineteen Home Demonstration Club members and Mr. Douglas A. Ducote, School Instructor, who learned to construct footstools to be woven with Hongkong Grass. Shown from left to right, front row are: Mrs. N. R. Ducote of Indian Bayou; Mrs. James Gauthier, Indian Bayou; Mrs. Thomas Ducote of Cottonport; Mrs. A. J. Aymond of Cottonport; Mrs. Lilly Koerkel of Mansura; Mrs. Adolph Gauthier of Indian Bayou; Mrs. A. M. Lemoine of Mansura; Mrs. Myrtice C. Juneau of Cottonport; Mrs. Vance Armand, Cottonport; and Miss Edna Mae Morris, Home Demonstration Agent.

Second Row, left to right: Mrs. Leonard Chenevert, Indian Bayou; Mrs. Herman J. Chatelain of Mansura; Mrs. Percy Brassette of Indian Bayou; Mrs. Gibbon Mayeux of Mansura; Mrs. Mary Ducote of Cottonport; Mrs. Adolph Bordelon of Indian Bayou; Mrs. Truby Chenevert of Cottonport; and Mrs. Felix Laborde of Mansura.

Back Row, left to right: Mrs. Allen Ducote of Indian Bayou and Mr. Douglas A. Ducote, Instructor for the Trade School.

Emma is shown fourth from the left on the front row.

The stool Emma made was graciously given to me by Kirk Aymond. I had the seat rewoven by a lady in Lafayette.

119

Best in Festival Bake-Off

By Elizabeth Norwood

Mrs. Arthur Aymond, Cottonport, La., captured the best-of-the-show yeast baking award, a $50 U. S. Saving bond and a gold ribbon, in the Louisiana Livestock and Pasture Festival held in Marksville, La. Her sweetheart coffee bread was judged the best, and with her entry, holiday bread, she, also, took home two blue ribbons.

Mrs. James Villemarette's loaf bread and dinner rolls brought her second honors. Others in the blue ribbon viewing of the award were Mrs. B. F. Lemoine, Hamburg, La., and Misses Mary K. Villemarette, Paula Moreau and Becky McClung, Marksville 4-H clubbers.

Homemade rolls and breads are becoming a favorite pastime for more families. Some 55 Avoyelles homemakers and 60 Junior division fanciers participated in the contest sponsored by the Home Demonstration council, Mrs. Maude Thevenot, Avoyelles HD agent, said.

Mrs. Aymond's winning recipes:

Basic Sweet Dough

2 packages active dry yeast, or 2 cakes compressed yeast
1¼ cups very warm water
1¼ teaspoons salt
½ cup water
3 tablespoons dry milk solids
3 eggs, beaten
2-3 cup melted shortening
6½ cups sifted flour

Sprinkle active dry yeast into very warm water. Stir until dissolved. Add salt, sugar, 2 cups flour and dry milk. Stir to blend, then beat well. Stir in eggs, then cooled melted shortening. Beat well. Stir in 4 more cups flour, reserving last ¼ cup for kneading. Sprinkle about ¼ cup flour on pastry cloth or board. Turn dough out in flour and knead until smooth and satiny (5 to 7 minutes), adding remaining ¼ cup flour if needed. Put dough into lightly greased bowl. Cover and let rise until doubled (about 1½ hours.) Punch down. Divide into portions for coffee cakes or rolls. Cover and let rest 5 minutes. Shape as desired.

Note: To store in refrigerator, cover bowl well and put in refrigerator immediately after dough is mixed and kneaded. Or store part of the dough in refrigerator. When wanted for baking, remove from refrigerator, punch down and shape breads and rolls. The dough will seem stiff at first, but it warms up and becomes pliable with handling. If only part of dough is needed, cut off required portion. Cover remaining portion well and put in refrigerator again.

Sweet Heart Coffee Bread

1-3 basic sweet dough recipe
1 tablespoon melted margarine or butter
¼ cup cinnamon-sugar

When dough is light, punch down. Let rest 5 minutes. Roll out into long narrow sheet ¼ inch thick and about 8 inches wide. Brush with melted margarine or butter, leaving one long edge unbrushed. Sprinkle Cinnamon-Sugar evenly over dough. Roll up to form long slender roll. Seal edge. Fold roll in half lengthwise. Press ends together. Place on greased baking sheet. Starting 1 inch from sealed ends cut lengthwise through center of dough. Form heart shape by turning cut ends out, and laying them flat on baking sheet. Let rise until doubled (about 45 minutes). Bake in moderate oven (350 degrees Fahrenheit) 25 to 30 minutes. When slightly cooled, decorate if desired with Confectioner's Sugar Frosting and chopped nuts.

Christmas Tree

1-3 basic sweet dough recipe
Confectioner's Sugar Frosting
Small colored candies
¼ cup shredded coconut

When dough is light, punch down. Divide into 3 or 4 parts. Let rest 5 minutes. Roll each part under hands to form long strands about ¾ inch in diameter. Starting with first strand, shape Christmas tree on greased baking sheet by weaving dough back and forth. Make each row of dough a little longer than the preceding one. Leave about ¼ inch space between rows of dough. Cut 3-inch length from last piece to make "trunk" of tree. Let rise until doubled (about 45 minutes). Bake in moderate oven (350 degrees Fahrenheit) 25 to 30 minutes. When cool, frost with Confectioner's Sugar Frosting and decorate with tiny colored candies. Sprinkle coconut on ends of "branches" to create snowy effect or use sliced candied cherries and pecan halves for decoration.

Confectioner's Sugar Icing

Mix together:
1 cup sifted confectioner's sugar
1 to 2 tablespoons warm water, milk or cream
(use amount for desired thickness)
½ teaspoon vanilla or lemon juice
(Use a bit of grated lemon rind with the lemon)

Mrs. Villemarette's Recipes:

Dinner Rolls

Mix together:
2 cups lukewarm milk
½ cup sugar
2 tsp. salt
Crumble into mixture:
2 cakes compressed yeast
Stir until yeast is dissolved
Stir in:
2 eggs
Mix in first with spoon:
½ cup soft shortening
Then hand:
7 to 7½ cups sifted flour
Add flour in 2 additions using

Mrs. Arthur Aymond, right, best baker in the annual Louisiana Livestock and Pasture Festival, proudly displays her winning entries with Mrs. James Villemarette, runnerup.

Emma's Apple Cake

1 ½ cups salad oil
2 cups sugar
2 eggs
2 tsp. vanilla
3 cups flour

1 tsp. salt
1 ¼ tsp. soda
3 apples peeled, cored, and chopped
½ cup pecans or walnuts

Mix together first 4 ingredients. Mix dry ingredients together and add to first mixture. Next, add apple pieces and pecans. Pour into greased tube pan and bake at 350 degrees for about one hour.

Oneal Aymond, Florida Aymond,
Arthur Aymond, Victoria Aymond,
and Leonce Aymond

Emma L. Aymond

Mrs. Emma Laborde Aymond, 91, of Cottonport died on May 15, 1980 at 6:00 at Rio Sol Nursing Home in Mansura. She was the widow of the late Arthur Aymond and a member of St. Marys Catholic Church Ladies Altar Society.

She is survived by three sons, Carol, Sr. and Herman, both of Cottonport and Burton of New Orleans; one daughter, Mrs. Odell Hanchey of Baton Rouge; one brother, Ludger of Baton Rouge; eleven grandchildren and sixteen great-grandchildren.

Funeral services were held in St. Marys Assumption Catholic Church in Cottonport by Msgr. Russell Ritchie and Wilfred Passchyn. Burial was in the church mausoleum under direction of Escude Funeral Home of Cottonport.

Herman and Odell

Standing: Herman and Carol
Sitting: Odell and Burton

Burton and his wife, Helena

Herman and wife, Pauline with
their son Billy

Burton and Helena Dauzat's wedding

L to R: Arthur, Emma, Burton, Helena, and Mr. & Mrs. Dauzat, Helena's parents

Buton and Helena on their honeymoon in Pensacola, Florida, June 2, 1957.

Burton and his son, Kirk, with the antique tractor that they restored together

Chapter 8: Carol James and Ordean Gaspard Aymond, Sr.

Carol Aymond, Sr. was born on July 14, 1921 in Cottonport, LA. He was the third of four children; Odel, Herman, Carol, and Burton. His parents were Arthur Aymond and Emma Laborde Aymond. His first home was the Laborde home of his grandparents in Indian Bayou.

Carol attended and graduated from Cottonport High School as did all five of his children. Also attending Cottonport High was Ordean Marie Gaspard who was to become his wife. Carol didn't particularly like school, but he excelled in math, going to the rally and placing second only because he, as a gentleman should, allowed a girl to turn in her paper before him. Following in his footsteps were two of his daughters who later became high school math teachers.

One of his childhood memories of living on Indian Bayou road was of his grandmother, Louise Gauthier. She had a small blue armoire made of beaded ceiling, which she kept on her back porch. She kept candy inside and kept it locked. He recalled that whenever he visited, she had candy for him.

When he was about a year old, his parents moved to Woodside, LA where his father was the overseer on the plantation owned by Pennican Ford. There, sugar cane was grown and shipped to the mill in Dora Bend (Hwy. 1184). They lived there for about two years and then moved back to Cottonport on Indian Bayou where they purchased Emma's family property for $3,000. (58 acres). His father farmed the property with 1 or 2 sharecroppers. They planted cotton, corn, and soybeans. They had one pair of mules called Bob and George to farm the property. At about the age of 8-9 he began working on the farm to clean water furrows with a shovel. Later, as he got older, he remembers plowing the fields with Bob and George. All the cotton was picked by hand and he remembers helping with this.

When he was about a year old, his parents move to Woodside, LA where his father was the overseer on the plantation owned by Pennican Ford. There, sugar cane was grown and shipped to the mill in Dora Bend (Hwy. 1184). They lived there for about two years and then moved back to Cottonport on Indian Bayou where they purchased Emma's family property for $3,000. (58 acres). His father farmed the property with 1 or 2 sharecroppers. They planted cotton, corn, and soybeans. They had one pair of mules called Bob and George to farm the property. At about the age of 8-9 he began working on the farm to clean water furrows with a shovel. Later, as he got older, he remembers plowing the fields with Bob and George. All the cotton was picked by hand and he remembers helping with this.

At about the age of seven, he began going to school in Cottonport. He walked to school daily with his brothers and sister. During this time, he came to know his high school sweetheart, Ordean Gaspard, who began attending Cottonport High in the 8th grade. Previously, she had been attending the elementary school in Dora Bend where they had multiple classes in one classroom. In 1941, they graduated together because she was allowed to skip a grade and he had begun later that the normal 6 years old.

Knowing that he was about to get drafted into service, on July 26, 1942, they were married at St. Mary's church in Cottonport, LA, by Father Gerard. He loved to tell the story about how he acquired his wedding suit. The suit that he wore on his wedding day was given to him by a Mr. Dodson. He had cut firewood for the gentleman who was unable to pay, so he offered the suit as payment. The suit, not being in the best of condition, had a hole in the back of the pants. His mother, Emma, patched the hole, and it became his wedding suit.

Mom's scholarship to Southwestern Louisiana after high school graduation. She always resented the fact that her brothers were allowed to go to college but as a girl, she was not.

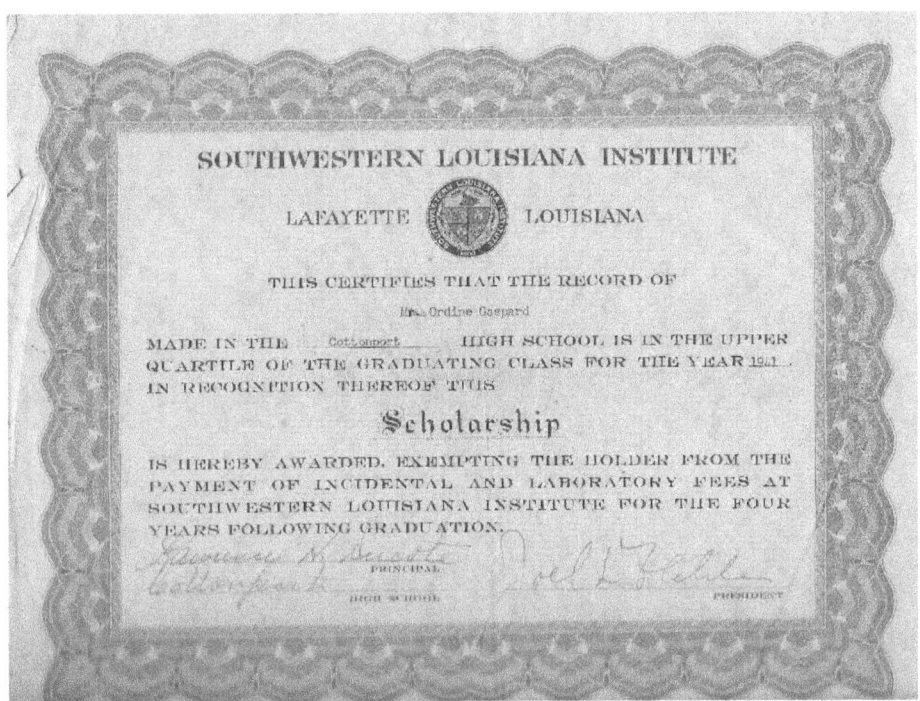

Carol and Ordean on their wedding day in Front of St. Mary's Catholic Church in Cottonport, LA, July 26, 1942

This is a picture of Carol on his wedding day with his parents, Arthur and Emma

126

Please Return to me.

Certificate of Marriage

✝

Church of

St. Mary's Assumption
Carlonpart, La

⊰ This is to Certify ⊱

That Carol James Aymond

and Ordeen Gaspard

were lawfully ⊰ Married ⊱

on the 26ᵗʰ day of July 19 42

According to the Rite of the Roman Catholic Church

and in conformity with the laws of the State of

Louisiana , Rev. J. Girard

officiating, in the presence of Currey Gaspard

and Lemay Gaspard, Amos Gaspard Witnesses, as appears

from the Marriage Register of this Church. Vol. II No. 5

Dated May 5, 1947

Rev. M. J. Broussard

Pastor

NO. 312 F. J. REMEY CO. INC. N.Y.

Husband: Carol James Aymond, Sr.
DOB: July 14, 1921 in Cottonport, LA
Died: December 18, 2016
Buried: Aymond Cemetery
      Cottonport, LA
Married: July 26, 1942
Where: St. Mary's Assumption Church
      Cottonport, LA
Parents: Arthur Aymond
      Emma Laborde

Wife: Ordean Marie Gaspard
DOB: January 21, 1925
Died: December 19, 2002
Buried: Aymond Cemetery,
      Indian Bayou Road
      Cottonport, LA
Parents: Landry Gaspard
      Mary Louise Descant

Children

Name	DOB - DOD	Married	Comments
Crystal Ann	6/5/1943	Terrell Guillory Bernie Suarez James Hedrick	She lived in Brandon, Florida until she married James Hedrick. They moved to Tennessee. She had three sons, Rhett, Randy, and Bernie, Jr.
Carol James, Jr.	10/23/1946	Donna Ducote Valentina Guzhvbinskaya.	He built a house on the bayou between Cottonport and Evergreen (Caro). He had two children, Carol (Jamie) Aymond, III and Chantel.
Darla Jean	12/27/47	Vance "Joey" Normand, Jr . Dillon Murchison	She lives in Baton Rouge, LA.. She had three children; Scott Normand, Amanda Normand, and Trent Murchison.
Martha Lynn	11/4/51	Christopher P. Bordelon	She lives in Dora Bend, between Cottonport and Evergreen. She and Chris had two daughters, Kristin and Rachel.
David Arthur	2/5/57	Susan Laborde	He lives in Madisonville, LA. He and Susan had five children; Leslie, Jennifer, Heather, Joshua, and Tyler.

A few months later, he enlisted in the Army Air Core. At the time, the Air Force was not a separate branch of service   After his enlistment, he was tested to determine his strengths.   It was found that he was mechanically inclined.   He attended basic training in Biloxi, MS in Keesler Field. He was then sent to Delgada in New Orleans for training in Aircrafts Mechanics and Electrical.

129

 ancestry

Carol J Aymond
in the U.S. World War II Army Enlistment Records, 1938-1946

Name:	Carol J Aymond
Birth Year:	1921
Race:	White, citizen (White)
Nativity State or Country:	Louisiana
State of Residence:	Louisiana
County or City:	Avoyelles
Enlistment Date:	13 Nov 1942
Enlistment State:	Louisiana
Enlistment City:	Lafayette
Branch:	Branch Immaterial - Warrant Officers, USA
Branch Code:	Branch Immaterial - Warrant Officers, USA
Grade:	Private
Grade Code:	Private
Term of Enlistment:	Enlistment for the duration of the War or other emergency, plus six months, subject to the discretion of the President or otherwise according to law
Component:	Selectees (Enlisted Men)
Source:	Civil Life
Education:	4 years of high school
Civil Occupation:	Semiskilled chauffeurs and drivers, bus, taxi, truck, and tractor
Marital Status:	Married
Height:	67
Weight:	144

Source Information

National Archives and Records Administration. *U.S. World War II Army Enlistment Records, 1938-1946* [database on-line]. Provo, UT, USA: Ancestry.com Operations Inc, 2005.

WAR DEPARTMENT
APPLICATION FOR FAMILY ALLOWANCES
(Servicemen's Dependents Allowance Act of 1942)

Do not write in this space
APPLICATION NUMBER
X-

(form, largely faded, with handwritten entries including "Aymond", "Carol", "James", "Private", "Barksdale Field, Mon.", "Married", "Male", "Cottonport, La.")

I. (a) Soldier ...

CLASS A

CLASS B DEPENDENTS

Make checks payable to—

Mrs. Ordean Marie Aymond, Cottonport, La.

This application provided a family allowance to be sent home to his wife, Ordean, while he was in service.

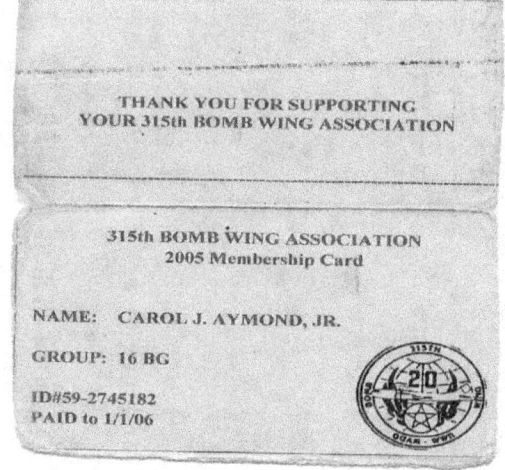

HEADQUARTERS Army Air Base, Abilene, Texas
Name CAROL J. AYMOND   38263438
Rank Sgt   Mos 685
Aviation Badge Authorized * * * * * * * * * * * *
Service Ribbons Authorized * * * * * * * * * * * *
Decoration Ribbons Authorized Good Conduct Ribbon,
Sharpshooter-Carbine, Mrkm.-Rifle,
JUL 15 1944
DATE   COMMANDING

THANK YOU FOR SUPPORTING
YOUR 315th BOMB WING ASSOCIATION

315th BOMB WING ASSOCIATION
2005 Membership Card

NAME: CAROL J. AYMOND, JR.

GROUP: 16 BG

ID#59-2745182
PAID to 1/1/06

Carol graduated from Delgada and was sent to Chanute Field in Rantoul and Champagne, Ill to specialize in Electrical. He later went to Nashville, TN to a plant where army planes were being built. He worked there for several weeks then was sent to Abilene, TX for more training. He remained there for several months. His wife, Ordean, joined him there with their young daughter, Crystal.

Orders came in for 3 aircraft electricians to go to Fairmont, NE. This is when he began training on B-29's. He was trained to set the engine and maintain the B29. From there, he left to go overseas to the Hawaiian Island, to Kwajalein Island (south of the equator) and then to Marianna Islands (Guam). He remained in Guam for about 9-10 months working on aircrafts. There were about 20 planes in the squadron on which he worked. The Northwest Field (Clark Airbase now) had about 500-600 planes. There was no highway to go into town, only a trail through the jungle. He remembers some of the planes that didn't come back from missions; some planes while trying to land, crashed. The plane on which he flew in was co-piloted by Major Campbell (they called him Soup-Campbell) who was the heir to Campbell Soup Company.

While he was there, he recalls the Japanese attempting to invade the Northwest Field. They failed because of the resistance that the navy provided. He recalls the Japanese on the island who, at times, would come out of the jungle. They lived below ground in tunnels and also with the natives on the island. The natives lived in grass huts. They planted rice patties and plowed their fields with the help of buffaloes.

When the war ended, he boarded a Landing Aircraft (LST) with 500 people. He said that it was the most miserable trip he had ever made. The vessel was a flat bottom one which made it extremely rough on the water. He remembers being sick for several days and remaining in his bunk. They could only wash-up with salty sea water, which was very irritable and made their hair "stand up". They stayed in Hawaii about 2 weeks for R & R. From there, he took a ship, the US Grant, and went to San Diego. He then traveled by train to Camp Fannin in Texas, where he was discharged from the Army.

Honorable Discharge Documents

Pictured below is the first house in which Carol, Ordean and their young daughter, Crystal, lived when he was discharged from service.

When he first returned to Cottonport, he and his wife lived with his mother-in-law for 6-8 months before getting their own place. Next, they lived in Crackville for about a year, before purchasing the property in Dora where they build a home. He recalls his mother-in-law, Mary Louise Descant Gaspard, not being very happy with him because he kept buying property instead of building her daughter a proper house. He knew that he had to make the investment in the property before building a house that would produce no revenue, only expenses.

Coming out of service, he had very little resources with which to make a living. Being a very resourceful and determined person, he lost no time in coming up with a plan. He bought a 2nd hand tractor from Mr. Rozas and a hay baler. He planted cotton at first that he and his wife picked. They would pick two bales of cotton in one week and then take the weekend off and start picking again on Monday. He recalls making very good use of his hay bailer, bailing hay for others in the area who didn't own a bailer.   He bailed hay from" sun-up to sun-down" and came back home in the dark. He said my mother would fix his lunch sandwich to bring with him in the morning, but he'd eat it on the way to the field because he didn't want to take the time to stop bailing at lunchtime.

Three years later he planted 2-3 acres of seed cane (sugar cane). The following year, he used this seed cane to plant a larger plot. He hired men to cut the cane by hand. Around 1950, he bought a new cane cutter to harvest his crop. From there, he bought more and more property as it became available. He continued to farm until he was 56 and then began renting out the property to local farmers. This allowed he and Ordean to do what they loved most, traveling.

Below is a bulletin from the Annual Sugar Cane Meeting on February 10, 1966. This bulletin lists Carol Aymond, Sr. as serving on the Sugar Cane Planning Committee.

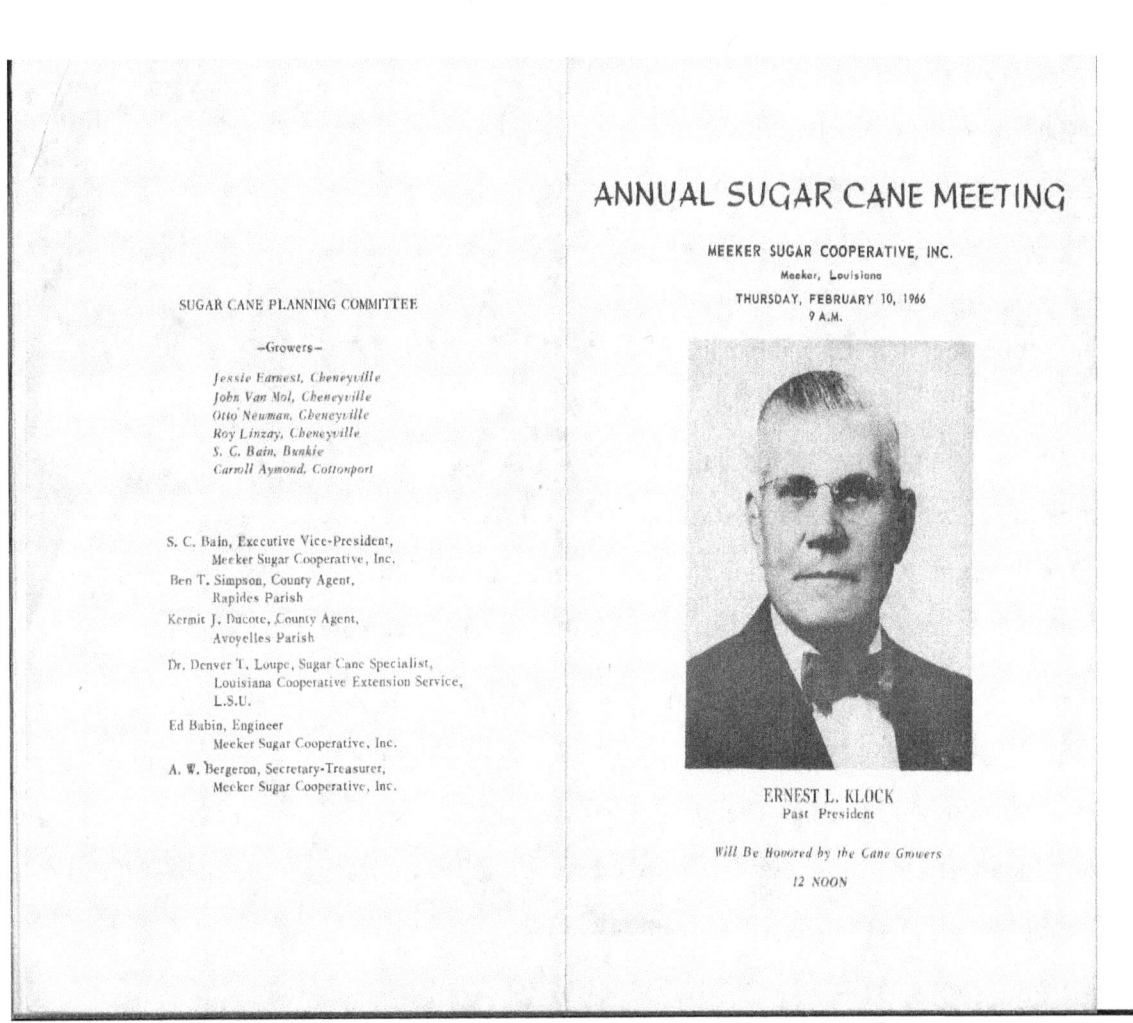

SUGAR CANE PLANNING COMMITTEE

—Growers—

Jessie Earnest, Cheneyville
John Van Mol, Cheneyville
Otto Neuman, Cheneyville
Roy Linzay, Cheneyville
S. C. Bain, Bunkie
Carroll Aymond, Cottonport

S. C. Bain, Executive Vice-President,
    Meeker Sugar Cooperative, Inc.
Ben T. Simpson, County Agent,
    Rapides Parish
Kermit J. Ducote, County Agent,
    Avoyelles Parish
Dr. Denver T. Loupe, Sugar Cane Specialist,
    Louisiana Cooperative Extension Service,
    L.S.U.
Ed Babin, Engineer
    Meeker Sugar Cooperative, Inc.
A. W. Bergeron, Secretary-Treasurer,
    Meeker Sugar Cooperative, Inc.

ANNUAL SUGAR CANE MEETING

MEEKER SUGAR COOPERATIVE, INC.
Meeker, Louisiana
THURSDAY, FEBRUARY 10, 1966
9 A.M.

ERNEST L. KLOCK
Past President

Will Be Honored by the Cane Growers

12 NOON

Carol and Ordean reared five children in Dora Bend. They all attended and graduated from Cottonport High School. After high school, he was determined that they all attend college so that they could have an "easier" life than he and my mother. There were no "ifs, ands, or buts" about it, you WERE going to go to college. He wanted his daughters to be teachers, a very safe and secure profession, and his sons were to be lawyers. So, unlike today, we all listened, except for me. I was determined NOT to be a teacher. So, I graduated in Business Administration instead. But, after I married and had two small children, and living in Cottonport, guess what??? I figured out that the only way to be home when my children were home, was to "teach". So, back to school to get a teaching degree. He didn't say, "I told you so.", but I could see it in his eyes!!

After we were all grown and gone, he and my mother traveled. There was nothing they liked better than packing up the car and heading out for parts unknown. They never really had a particular destination in mind, they just like to "go". They traveled to all the states except Alaska. They also visited Canada, Nova Scotia, St. Edward Island and New Brunswick. My mother particularly like to eat at Wendy's. Dad always said he could find a Wendy's without a map in any state in which he found himself!

One particular item which he loved to collect was old school/church bells. He had a large collection of them from different parts of the United States. The largest one that he had, he located in Tennessee. It was 48 inches in diameter. He decided that he would build a tower on which to mount the bell. Under the tower, he constructed a granite memorial to his  family. On the tower appears his and my mother's names and also the names of their children. It can still be seen at their home place on Highway 1184 between Evergreen and Cottonport.

My mother, Ordean Gaspard Aymond, died in 2001 at age 76 due to complication from Alzheimer's Disease. She is buried in the Aymond Cemetery on the Indian Bayou Road in Cottonport. My dad died on December 18, 2016. He was 95 years old. He was a resident of Oak Mont Estates, an assisted living facility in Mansura, LA. He remained very active until he was 93. He still drove his car wherever he wanted, oftentimes getting speeding tickets.

ORDEAN GASPARD AYMOND

Services for Ordean Gaspard Aymond were at 3:00 pm Thursday, Dec. 20, 2002 in St. Mary Assumption Catholic Church with Fr. Matt Wollett officiating. Entombment was in the Aymond Cemetery, Cottonport under direction of Melançon Funeral Home, Bunkie.

Mrs. Aymond, age 76, of Cottonport expired on Wednesday, Dec. 19, 2002 in Avoyelles Hospital, Marksville.

Survivors include her husband Carol Aymond, Sr. of Cottonport; two sons Carol Aymond, Jr. of Bunkie and David Aymond of Mandeville; three daughters Crystal Hedrick of Sevierville, TN, Darla Aymond of Mandeville and Martha Bordelon of Cottonport; one sister Verda Nugent of Jackson, MS; 14 grandchildren and 7 great grandchildren.

Pallbearers were Chris Bordelon, Chad Gaspard, Drew Maciasz, Keith Gaspard, Jason Normand, Kirk Aymond, Josh Aymond, Scotty Normand and Trent Murchison.

Friends called at St. Mary's from 1:30 pm until service time on Thursday, Dec. 20, 2002.

On Eagle's Wings

And He will raise you up
on eagle's wings,
Bear you on the
breath of dawn,
Make you to shine
like the sun,
And hold you in the
palm of His hand.

—Michael Joncas

Carol Aymond, Sr.
July 14, 1921 – December 18, 2016

A Mass of Christian Burial was offered for Carol Aymond, Sr. on Tuesday, December 20, 2016 at 11:00 a.m. at St. Mary's Assumption Catholic Church in Cottonport with Fr. Jose Robles-Sanchez officiating. Burial with Military Honors was in the Aymond Family Cemetery on Indian Bayou Road in Cottonport under the direction of Melancon Funeral Home, Bunkie. Visitation was at St. Mary's Assumption Catholic Church on Tuesday, December 20, 2016 from 9:00 a.m. - 10:45 a.m. Mr. Aymond, age 95, of Cottonport, passed away on Sunday, December 18, 2016 at OakMont Estates. He was born on July 14, 1921 in Cottonport, LA. He was the 3rd of four children; Odel, Herman, Carol, and Burton. His parents were Arthur Aymond and Emma Laborde Aymond. He married his high school sweetheart, Ordean Marie Gaspard, on July 26, 1942. He and Ordean bought a portion of Dora Plantation where they built their home and reared their five children. Carol served in the United States Army Air Corps (USAAC), which was a forerunner of the U.S. Air Force. He attended basic training in Biloxi, MS at Keesler Air Force Base. He later graduated from Delgado School in New Orleans as an aircraft electrician and mechanic. He trained on B29's in Fairmont, NE before going overseas to the Hawaiian Islands and then to Guam where he worked on aircrafts. When the war ended, Carol received an honorable discharge from the U.S. Army Air Corps. He returned to Cottonport and his family and began farming. He grew sugarcane and served on the board of the Meeker Sugar Co-Op. He farmed until he retired at age 56. Preceding him in death were his wife, Ordean Gaspard Aymond, his parents Arthur and Emma Aymond, his brother Herman Aymond, his sister Odel Hanchey, and his grandchild Bernard Suarez, Jr. Carol was a devoted husband, father, and grandfather. He will be greatly missed by all his family and friends. Survivors include his brother Burton Aymond of Metairie, and his children and their spouses; Crystal Hedrick and husband James of Sevierville, TN, Carol, Aymond, Jr. of Bunkie, Darla Aymond of Mandeville, Martha and husband Chris Bordelon of Cottonport, and David Aymond and his wife Susan of Madisonville. Carol and Ordean had 15 grandchildren; Randy Aymond, Rhett Suarez, Carol Aymond, III, Chantel Aymond, Scott Normand, Amanda Maciasz, Trent Murchison, Kristin Normand, Rachel Normand, Delilah Aymond, Leslie Aymond, Jennifer Picone, Joshua Aymond, Heather Aymond and Tyler Aymond. He also had 21 great-grandchildren. During their retirement years, Carol and Ordean always loved to travel. They were never happier than when planning a road trip. Ordean's hobby was genealogy and they traveled all over the United States to many churches, cemeteries, and other out-of-the-way places seeking information on their ancestors.
www.melanconfunerals.com

Melancon Funeral Home – Bunkie, LA

136

Ordean, Carol, and David

Ordean and Carol with a B-59 plane

Carol Aymond, Sr. with his daughters, Martha and Darla, on his 94th birthday. His gift from them was memorabilia from his time spent in service during WWII.

The five children of Carol and Ordean Aymond: Then and Later

Darla, Crystal, Martha, Carol, Jr., and David

Front: Crystal, Martha, & Darla   Back row: David and Carol, Jr.

Mom and Dad and their "Little Red Jeep"!

The "Bell Tower", constructed by Carol J. Aymond, Sr. It is located on their home place on Highway 1184, Cottonport, where Carol and Ordean reared their family of five children.

139

Carol Aymond, Sr., WWII vet and Cottonport farmer dies at age 95

COTTONPORT- A Mass of Christian Burial for Carol Aymond, Sr. was held on Tuesday, December 20, 2016, at 11 a.m. at St. Mary's Assumption Catholic Church in Cottonport where Fr. Jose Robles-Sanchez officiated. Burial followed with military honors in the Aymond Family Cemetery on Indian Bayou Road in Cottonport under the direction of Melancon Funeral Home, Bunkie.

Aymond, age 95, of Cottonport, passed away on Sunday, December 18, 2016, at OakMont Estates.

He was born on July 14, 1921 in Cottonport. He was the third of four children: Odel, Herman, Carol, and Burton. His parents were Arthur Aymond and Emma

bought a portion of Dora Plantation where they built their home and reared their five children.

Carol served in the United States Army Air Corps (USAAC), which was a forerunner of the U.S. Air Force during World War II. He attended basic training in Biloxi, Mississippi at Keesler Air Force Base. He later graduated from Delgada School in New Orleans as an aircraft electrician and mechanic. He trained on B29's in Fairmont, Nebraska before going overseas to the Hawaiian Islands and then to Guam where he worked on aircrafts.

When the war ended, Carol received an honorable discharge from the U.S. Army Air Corps. He returned to Cottonport and

Carol Aymond, Sr.

until he retired at age 56.

During their retirement years, Carol and Ordean always loved to travel. They were never happier than when planning a road trip. Ordean's hobby was genealogy and they traveled all over the United States to many churches,

were his wife, Ordean Gaspard Aymond; his parents Arthur and Emma Aymond; his brother Herman Aymond; his sister Odel Hanchey; and his grandchild, Bernard Suarez, Jr.

Survivors include his brother, Burton Aymond of Metairie; and his five children, Crystal (James) Hedrick of Sevierville, Tennessee, Carol Aymond, Jr. of Bunkie, Darla Aymond of Mandeville, Martha (Chris) Bordelon of Cottonport, and David (Susan) Aymond of Madisonville; 15 grandchildren; Randy Aymond, Rhett Suarez, Carol Aymond, III, Chantel Aymond, Scott Normand, Amanda Maciasz, Trent Murchison, Kristin Normand, Rachel Normand, Delilah

STATE OF LOUISIANA
CERTIFICATION OF VITAL RECORD

CERTIFICATION OF DEATH

BIRTH NUMBER:

STATE FILE NUMBER: 2016-042-00513

5358298

DECEDENT	DECEDENT'S NAME - (LAST, FIRST, MIDDLE, SUFFIX)	DATE OF BIRTH	DATE OF DEATH	TIME OF DEATH
	AYMOND SR , CAROL JAMES	07/14/1921	12/16/2016	02:18 AM
	PLACE OF BIRTH - (CITY, STATE, COUNTRY)	SEX	SOCIAL SECURITY NUMBER	AGE
	COTTONPORT, LA UNITED STATES	MALE	434-22-9245	95 YEARS
	DECEDENT'S ALIAS NAME(S) - (LAST, FIRST, MIDDLE, SUFFIX):			

	RESIDENCE OF DECEDENT - (STREET ADDRESS, CITY, STATE, ZIP CODE, COUNTRY)		WITHIN CITY LIMITS?	PARISH/COUNTY
	1781 HWY 1184 , COTTONPORT, LA 71327 UNITED STATES		NO	AVOYELLES

PERSONAL	EVER IN U.S. ARMED FORCES?	OCCUPATION	INDUSTRY OF OCCUPATION
	YES	FARMER	AGRICULTURE
	MARITAL STATUS		NAME OF SURVIVING SPOUSE (LAST, FIRST, MIDDLE, SUFFIX)
	WIDOWED		
	FATHER/PARENT NAME - (LAST, FIRST, MIDDLE, SUFFIX)		FATHER/PARENT PLACE OF BIRTH - (CITY, STATE, COUNTRY)
	AYMOND, ARTHUR		PLAUCHEVILLE, LA UNITED STATES
	MOTHER/PARENT NAME - (LAST, FIRST, MIDDLE, SUFFIX)		MOTHER/PARENT PLACE OF BIRTH - (CITY, STATE, COUNTRY)
	LABORDE, EMMA		COTTONPORT, LA UNITED STATES

	INFORMANT'S NAME - (LAST, FIRST, MIDDLE, SUFFIX)	RELATIONSHIP TO DECEDENT	INFORMANT'S ADDRESS
	BORDELON, MARTHA AYMOND	DAUGHTER	1661 HWY 1184 , COTTONPORT, LA 71327 UNITED STATES

EDUCATION: HIGH SCHOOL GRADUATE, OR GED COMPLETED

OF HISPANIC ORIGIN?: NO, NOT SPANISH/HISPANIC/LATINO

RACE: WHITE

DEATH INFO	PLACE OF DEATH	FACILITY NAME
	OTHER OAKMONT ESTATES	
	FACILITY ADDRESS - (STREET ADDRESS, CITY, STATE, ZIP CODE, COUNTRY)	PARISH/COUNTY
	204 COCOVILLE RD. , MANSURA, LA 71350 UNITED STATES	AVOYELLES

DISPOSITION	METHOD OF DISPOSITION	PLACE OF DISPOSITION
	BURIAL	AYMOND FAMILY CEMETERY
	PLACE OF DISPOSITION - (CITY, STATE, COUNTRY)	DATE OF DISPOSITION
	COTTONPORT, LA UNITED STATES	12/20/2016

FUNERAL FACILITY	FUNERAL FACILITY NAME	ADDRESS OF FUNERAL FACILITY
	MELANCON FUNERAL HOME, INC - BUNKIE	108 N. LEXINGTON AVE. , BUNKIE, LA 71522 UNITED STATES
	NAME OF FUNERAL DIRECTOR (LAST, FIRST, MIDDLE, SUFFIX)	LICENSE NUMBER	CORONER NOTIFIED?
	MELANCON, MARJORIE B	U1190	Y
	SIGNATURE OF FUNERAL DIRECTOR	DATE
	e-sign	1/4/2017

MEDICAL INFO	MANNER OF DEATH	NATURAL
	IF FEMALE?	NOT APPLICABLE
	DID TOBACCO USAGE CONTRIBUTE TO DEATH?	UNKNOWN

CAUSE OF DEATH	PART I. Enter the chain of events – diseases, injuries, or complications – that directly caused the death. DO NOT enter terminal events such as cardiac arrest, respiratory arrest, or ventricular fibrillation without showing the etiology. DO NOT ABBREVIATE.		APPROXIMATE INTERVAL: Onset to Death
	IMMEDIATE CAUSE - (Final disease or condition resulting in death)	a. CONGESTIVE HEART FAILURE	UNK
	Sequentially list conditions, if any, leading to the cause listed on line a	b.	
	Enter the UNDERLYING CAUSE (disease or injury that initiated the events resulting in death) LAST	c.	
		d.	

PART II. Enter other significant conditions contributing to death but not resulting in the underlying cause given in PART I.

HYPERTENSION/A FIB/PROSTATE CANCER

	WAS AN AUTOPSY PERFORMED?	FINDINGS USED IN DETERMINING CAUSE?
	NO	NOT APPLICABLE

INJURY INFORMATION	PLACE OF INJURY	DATE OF INJURY	TIME OF INJURY	INJURY AT WORK	IF TRANSPORTATION INJURY, SPECIFY:
	LOCATION OF INJURY - (STREET ADDRESS, CITY, STATE, ZIP CODE, COUNTRY)				PARISH/COUNTY
	DESCRIBE HOW INJURY OCCURRED				

CERTIFIER	I CERTIFY THIS 'CORONER CASE' BASED ON MY EXAMINATION OR INVESTIGATION AND, IN MY OPINION, DEATH OCCURRED AT THE TIME, DATE, AND PLACE, AND DUE TO THE CAUSE(S) AND MANNER STATED.		
	SIGNATURE OF CERTIFIER	*e-sign*	DATE	1/3/2017
	CERTIFIER NAME - (LAST, FIRST, MIDDLE, SUFFIX)	MAYEUX, LOVELL J		
	CERTIFIER TITLE: CORONER			
	CERTIFIER ADDRESS - (STREET ADDRESS, CITY, STATE, ZIP CODE, COUNTRY)			
	1444 S. MAIN ST. , MARKSVILLE, LA 71351 UNITED STATES			

	BURIAL TRANSIT PERMIT	PARISH OF ISSUE	DATE OF ISSUE	DATE FILED WITH REGISTRAR
				1/4/2017

REGISTRAR	SIGNATURE OF REGISTRAR	DEVIN GEORGE *e-sign*

ISSUED BY: Stafford, LaKeytha N

Issued On: 1/6/2017 9:17:25 AM

005358298

I CERTIFY THAT THIS IS A TRUE AND CORRECT COPY OF A CERTIFICATE OR DOCUMENT REGISTERED WITH THE VITAL RECORDS REGISTRY OF THE STATE OF LOUISIANA, PURSUANT TO LSA - R.S. 40:32, ET SEQ.

A REPRODUCTION OF THIS DOCUMENT IS VOID AND INVALID.
DO NOT ACCEPT

DEVIN GEORGE
STATE REGISTRAR

Chapter 9: Carol James Aymond, Jr.

Carol Aymond, Jr. was born in Cottonport, LA on   October 23, 1946. His parents were Carol Aymond, Sr. and   Ordean Marie Gaspard Aymond. He grew up on Bayou Rouge,   Dora Bend, a community between Evergreen and   Cottonport.   He was the second of five children.

Carol, like his brothers and sisters, graduated from Cottonport High School. As young boy, Carol, called Pierre by his friends, helped his father on the sugarcane farm driving a tractor. He also enjoyed riding   his quarter horse, Sally. He would ride Sally a mile   down   Hwy 1184 from where he lived, to race at "Dora Downs".   This was where local people brought their horses on lazy   Sunday afternoons for fun and friendly betting. He   and his   horse often won the races in which they competed.

Carol attended Cottonport High School for grades 1-12, and graduated in 1964. He was a member of the Beta Club, participated in sports, was the Louisiana State Soil Judging Champion in 1963, and was a member of the International Soil Judging Team in 1964. From 1964 to 1968, he attended Louisiana State University in Baton Rouge, where he was selected in 1965 as the Outstanding Freshman in the College of Agriculture and was awarded the Dan Ford Foundation Award for national recognition.

The American Youth Foundation

For the Christian Leadership Training
of American Youth

3460 Hampton Ave., St. Louis, Mo. 63139

April 21, 1965

Dear Carol:

I wish to congratulate you on the honor that has come to you in being selected as one of the delegates to receive the William H. Danforth scholarship to Camp Miniwanca. You will have the opportunity of camping, fellowship, and training with outstanding young people from all parts of the continent, and I am sure you are looking forward with pleasure to this challenging experience.

In confirmation of your registration, please fill out and return the enclosed pre-camp blank. The information it contains will help us in planning for camp, and cabin assignments will be made from these sheets. It will help us if you will return the blank promptly.

Early in July you will receive complete instructions regarding travel, camp plans, and an equipment list. In the meantime, I want you to know how glad we are that you can be with us, and we extend you a hearty welcome into our friendly Miniwanca circle.

Sincerely yours,

William P. Oliver, Jr.

William P. Oliver, Jr.
Director

Camp dates: Older Girls - August 2 to 15
Older Boys - August 16 to 29

Carol married his high school sweetheart, Donna Ducote on July 22, 1967 at St. Joseph's Catholic Church in Beaumont, Texas. Donna had family living in Cottonport and often visited the small town. Her cousin, Butch, was one of Carol's good friends, thus, she became acquainted with Carol. She was the daughter of Mr. and Mrs. Terry Ducote of Beaumont, Texas. Not having a vehicle, he often "hitchhiked" to Beaumont to visit her on the weekends. Carol and Donna had two children, Carol "Jamie" Aymond, III and Chantel Aymond. .

In 1968, Carol graduated in Agricultural Business from LSU and was accepted into Loyola University School of Law in New Orleans, La.

In 1969, he was drafted into the U.S. Military. Upon completion of Basic Training and Advanced Infantry Training at Fort Polk, Louisiana; he was selected to attend Non- Commissioned Officer's School in Fort Benning, Georgia, for advanced Infantry Training. He then returned to Fort Polk as an NCO Officer to train infantry soldiers preparing for duty and assignment in Vietnam. (Pictured with his mother, Ordean G. Aymond)

He participated in the Vietnam Campaign from 1970-71 as an NCO with the First Aircraft Infantry Unit, where he served in the Vietnam Jungles as combat infantry NCO Officer through 1971. Of said service, Carol was awarded the Bronze Star.

Citation

BY DIRECTION OF THE PRESIDENT

THE BRONZE STAR MEDAL

IS PRESENTED TO

SERGEANT CAROL J. AYMOND   437705305

UNITED STATES ARMY

who distinguished himself by outstandingly meritorious service in connection with military operations against a hostile force in the Republic of Vietnam. During the period

SEPTEMBER 1970 TO MAY 1971

he consistently manifested exemplary professionalism and initiative in obtaining outstanding results. His rapid assessment and solution of numerous problems inherent in a combat environment greatly enhanced the allied effectiveness against a determined and aggressive enemy. Despite many adversities, he invariably performed his duties in a resolute and efficient manner. Energetically applying his sound judgment and extensive knowledge, he has contributed materially to the successful accomplishment of the United States mission in the Republic of Vietnam. His loyalty, diligence and devotion to duty were in keeping with the highest traditions of the military service and reflect great credit upon himself and the United States Army.

Separation from the Army

DEPARTMENT OF THE ARMY
HEADQUARTERS, 3RD BRIGADE (SEPARATE)
1ST CAVALRY DIVISION (AIRMOBILE)
APO San Francisco 96490

SPECIAL ORDERS
NUMBER   14   23 April 1971
EXTRACT

30. TC 206. Following individuals reassigned to Transfer Station or Transfer
Point for separation processing and will proceed on PERMANENT CHANGE OF STATION
as indicated below.

FLANAGAN, CHARLES D 258789046 SP4 11B20 HHC 3rd Bde WAGHAAA
HOR: 405 Atlanta St., Barnsville, GA PL EAD or OAD: Atlanta, GA
SPN: 411 ETS: 22 Sep 71 Component: AUS DEROS: 27 Apr 71 DDUS: 6 Apr 70

SMITH, ROSE 226728326 SP4 63K20 Det 3, HHC 3rd Bde WAGHAAA-D
HOR: PO Box 1061, Quincy, Florida PL EAD or OAD: Jacksonville, Florida
SPN: 411 ETS: 16 Jun 71 Component: AUS DEROS: 25 Apr 71 DDUS: 18 Jun 70
54 Day curtailment of FST is directed IAW USARV MSG 030716Z Mar 71

CRASK, JAMES G 309588419 SP4 31B20 Det 2, HHC 3rd Bde WAGHAAA-C
HOR: 624 E Virginia, Evansville, Indiana PL EAD or OAD: Louisville, Kentucky
SPN: 411 ETS: 9 Sep 71 Component: AUS DEROS: 26 Apr 71 DDUS: 24 Mar 70

WILLIAMS, ALFRED 332380152 SP4 05C20 Det 7, HHC 3rd Bde WAGHAAA-H
HOR: 1251 S Fairfield, Chicago, Illinois PL EAD or OAD: Chicago, Illinois
SPN: 411 ETS: 21 Sep 71 Component: AUS DEROS: 2 May 71 DDUS: 11 Jun 70
39 Day curtailment of FST is directed.

GRAHAM, LEE O 441424151 SSG 11B40 HHC 2nd Bn 5th Cav WAGMTOA
HOR: 2736 NW 21st St, Oklahoma City, Oklahoma PL EAD or OAD: Oklahoma City, OK
SPN: 411 ETS: 18 Jun 71 Component: AUS DEROS: 2 May 71 DDUS: 12 Jun 70
40 Day curtailment of FST is directed.

PFEIFF, EDWARD J 368565631 SGT 11C40 Co B 1st Bn 12th Cav WAGUBOA
HOR: RR 1, Box 195, Stephenson, Michigan PL EAD or OAD: Milwaukee, Wisconsin
SPN: 411 ETS: 11 Jun 71 Component: AUS DEROS: 29 Apr 71 DDUS: 19 Jun 70
39 Day curtailment of FST is directed.

GROOTERS, RICHARD W 471624847 SGT 11F40 Co B 2nd Bn 5th Cav WAGMBOA
HOR: Lime Springs, Iowa PL EAD or OAD: Minneapolis, Minnesota
SPN: 411 ETS: 15 Jun 71 Component: RA DEROS: 1 May 71 DDUS: 22 Jun 70
38 Day curtailment of FST is directed.

ERSTAD, MARVIN L 468563623 SGT 11D40 Co D 2nd Bn 5th Cav WAGMDOA
HOR: 607 W Main St, Ada, Minnesota PL EAD or OAD: Fargo, North Dakota
SPN: 411 ETS: 23 Jun 71 Component: AUS DEROS: 29 Apr 71 DDUS: 5 Jun 70
37 Day curtailment of FST is directed.

JENKINS, EDWARD E 249928020 SGT 11B40 Co D 2nd Bn 5th Cav WAGMDOA
HOR: 371/2 Hillside Ave, Lancaster, North Carolina PL EAD or OAD: Charlotte, NC
SPN: 411 ETS: 10 Jun 71 Component: DEROS: 28 Apr 71 DDUS: 12 Jun 70
39 Day curtailment of FST is directed.

Para 30 SO 14 DA HQ 3rd Bde (Sep) 1st Cav Div (AM) APO S.F. 96490 23 Apr 71 Cont:

MEREDITH, TERRANCE D 333442432 SP4 11B20 Co C 2nd Bn 8th Cav WAGRCOA
HOR: RR 2, Jerseyville, Illinois PL EAD or OAD: St Louis, Missouri
SPN: 411 ETS: 4 Aug 71 Component: AUS DEROS: 30 Apr 71 DDUS: 8 Jul 70
38 Day curtailment of FST is directed.

AYMOND, CAROL J Jr 437705305 SGT 11B40 Co B 2nd Bn 8th Cav WAGRBOA
HOR: 2440 S 9th St, Beaumont, Texas PL EAD or OAD: New Orleans, Louisiana
SPN: 411 ETS: 23 Jun 71 Component: AUS DEROS: 30 Apr 71 DDUS: 8 Jun 70
39 Day curtailment of FST is directed.

ADMINISTRATIVE ACCOUNTING DATA
Authority: AR 635-200
Maj Comd/Agcy: USARV
PCS MDC: 5DE1
PC Cont No: NA
CIC: 211A03

FOR THE INDIVIDUAL
Assigned to: US Army Transfer Station, Oakland, California 94626
Reporting date: NA
Port call data: NA
Availability date: NA
Special Instructions: (a) Comply with the following numbered items of
DA Sup Instr (App B, AR 310-10): 36, 39, 58, 62, 65.
(b) Comply with the following items of 3d Bde (Sep), 1st
Cav Div Sup Instr: A, B, C.
(c) The carrying of any kind of dangerous articles
(hand grenades, tear gas grenades, signal kits, etc.),
firearms ammunition, explosive or incendiary ammunition, or any kind of explosive device in accompanied
or unaccompied personal baggage aboard military aircraft is prohibited.
(d) Report to the (22d or 90th) Repl Bn NST 72 hours prior
to deros and NLT 0900 hours the day prior to deros.

FOR THE COMMANDER:

OFFICIAL:

L. B. MINEWEASER
CPT, AGC
Asst AG

JOHN W. KLINGELHOEFER
LTC, FA
Executive Officer

DISTRIBUTION:
35 - AG Orders Br
25 - Each Indiv Conc
55 - AVDAFI-C
2 - Co C 2nd Bn 8th Cav
2 - Det 3, HHC 3rd Bde
2 - Det 7, HHC 3rd Bde
2 - Co B 1st Bn 12th Cav
2 - Co D 2nd Bn 5th Cav

10 - AOR Out Proc
165 - AVDAAG-R
2 - Co B 2nd Bn 8th Cav
2 - HHC 3rd Bde
2 - Det 2, HHC 3rd Bde
2 - HHC 2nd Bn 5th Cav
2 - Co B 2nd Bn 5th Cav
5 - USATRFSTA, Oakland, California
(For MR & Admin Pur)

Upon completion of his military service, Carol returned to Loyola Law School from which he graduated in 1973. He began an associate practice with Alfred A. Mansour in Alexandria from 1973-75.

In 1975, he moved back to Avoyelles Parish where he and his wife, Donna, built a home. He began an active practice in personal injury law until his retirement in 1999. As an attorney in Avoyelles Parish, Carol was often involved in community affairs. He served as judge in the Towns of Cottonport, Simmesport, Mansura and Hessmer. He also ran for Division A City Judge in Avoyelles Parish in 1978. Carol practiced personal injury law on a full-time basis as well as being active in community service and farming with his father. Since his retirement from personal injury law practice, he has had the opportunity to practice before the United States Supreme Court and most all Louisiana courts in every judicial district in the state.

148

Please Support

Carol J.

AYMOND, JR.

As Your Judge -- Division "A"

#48

As Your Judge:

1. I believe that DRUGS are destroying our parish; it can and will be stopped.

2. Drug pushers will do the time for the crime without parole.

3. The courtroom will be free of politics and everyone will be treated fairly and equally.

4. Problem children need to be sent to a military type boot camp school and not suspended and put on the streets.

5. Our senior citizens need to be protected and made safe in their homes and streets.

6. I will support the neighborhood school concept.

7. Treat everyone with an open door and mind, a fair hearing, courtesy and respect, and a smile.

8. The right of teachers to discipline children.

9. Your constitutional right to bear arms.

10. The duty and obligation of all parents to support and discipline their children.

11. As a cattleman and farmer for many years, I understand your particular problems.

ON SEPTEMBER 21, 1996, YOU CAN MAKE A POSITIVE CHANGE IN AVOYELLES PARISH - - - PLEASE VOTE TO ELECT

CAROL J. AYMOND, JR.

#48, As Your Judge, Division "A"

Paid for by Committee to Elect Carol J. Aymond, Jr., Chairman, Janet Geal

After retiring from his law practice, Carol decided to travel to Russia. It was during this visit that he met Valentina Guzhvbinskaya. After returning home, he and "Val" corresponded through e-mail. He decided to go back to Russia to visit Val again. They decided to marry during this time, and thus began the arduous task of legally getting Val back to the U.S. to be married. They were married on December 29, 2006 in Long Pine, Louisiana.

Val had a daughter, Margarita Vladiminovna who was ten years old when they moved to Louisiana. "Rita" quickly became accustomed to the U.S. lifestyle and attended school at St. Mary's Catholic School in Cottonport, later she attended and graduated from Avoyelles Public Charter School. From there, she moved to Baton Rouge to attend Louisiana State University.

On June 4, 2011, Carol and Val were blessed with the birth of their child, Delila. His marriage to Val, later ended in divorce.

Husband: Carol James Aymond, Jr.
DOB: October 23, 1946
Died:
Buried:
Married: July 22, 1967
Where: St. Joseph's Catholic Church, Beaumont, TX
Father: Carol J. Aymond, Sr. (1921)
Mother: Ordean Gaspard

Wife: Donna Ducote
DOB: May 30,
Died:
Buried:

Father: Terry Ducote
Mother: Georgette Gaillard
      (7/16/1923-10/15/1964)

Children:

Name	DOB - DOD	Married	Comments
Carol James "Jamie" Aymond	DOB: Feb. 14, 1970	Deborah Bruner	Lived in LaGrange, TX
Chantel Aymond	DOB: 1975		Lived in Houston, TX

Married: December 29, 2006
Where: Long Pine, LA
Father: Vladimir Stepanovich Guzhvinskiy
     (born in Snobodniy)
Mother: Valentina Alexeevna Grehova
     Guzhvinskaya (born in Novosibirsk)

Wife: Valentina Vladimirovna Guzhvinskaya
DOB: April 20,

Children:

Name	DOB - DOD	Married	Comments
Deliah	6/4/2011		Born in Lafayette, LA

151

Certificate of Baptism

I hereby certify, that _Carol James Jr. Aymond_
Son of _Carol James Aymond_ and _Ardin Marie Lager_
was born in _Bunkie, La._ on the _23rd_ day of _October_ 1946
and was Baptized according to the Rite of the Roman Catholic Church
on the _9th_ day of _November_ 1946 by Rev. _J. Girard_
the Sponsors being _Lumpter Guthies_ and _Minnie Laborde_
as appears in the Register of the Church.

Dated _____ 19___   _J. Girard_   Pastor

L. N. Daleiden & Co. Pub., Chicago, Ill.

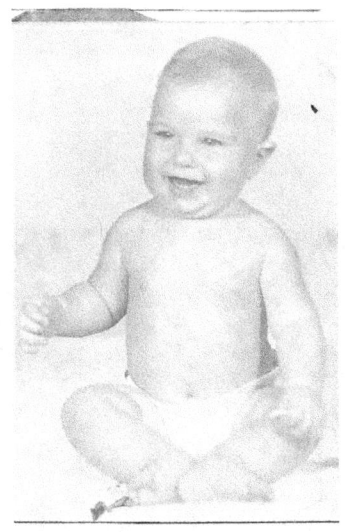

Carol, Jr. at 8 months

SCHOOL DAYS 1957-'58
Cottonport

Carol, Jr. age 12

Carol, Jr. and Martha

with his horse, Sally.

Pictured are Carol Aymond, III, his two children, Julia Rose and Weston,

and his sister, Chantel Aymond

Weston, Carol Aymond, III,
Carol Aymond, Sr., and Julia
taken in 2016

153

DEPARTMENT OF STATE HEALTH SERVICES
VITAL STATISTICS

TEXAS DEPARTMENT OF STATE HEALTH SERVICES - VITAL STATISTICS
Mar 12 2021

STATE OF TEXAS	CERTIFICATE OF DEATH	STATE FILE NUMBER 142-21-052784	2. DATE OF DEATH - ACTUAL OR PRESUMED (mm-dd-yyyy)
		(Before Marriage)	FEBRUARY 26, 2021

1. LEGAL NAME OF DECEASED (Include AKA's, if any) (First, Middle, Last)
CARROLL JAMES AYMOND JR.

3. SEX	4. DATE OF BIRTH (mm-dd-yyyy)	5. AGE-Last Birthday (Years)	IF UNDER 1 YR Mo / Days	IF UNDER 1 DAY Hours / Min	6. BIRTHPLACE (City & State or Foreign Country)
MALE	OCTOBER 23, 1946	74			UNKNOWN, LA

7. SOCIAL SECURITY NUMBER	8. MARITAL STATUS AT TIME OF DEATH	9. SURVIVING SPOUSE'S NAME (If spouse, give name prior to first marriage)
437-70-5305	☐ Married ☐ Widowed (but not remarried) ☒ Divorced (but not remarried) ☐ Never Married ☐ Unknown	

10a. RESIDENCE STREET ADDRESS	10b. APT. NO.	10c. CITY OR TOWN
3723 HIGHWAY 29		EVERGREEN

10d. COUNTY	10e. STATE	10f. ZIP CODE	10g. INSIDE CITY LIMITS?
AVOYELLES	LOUISIANA	71333	☐ Yes ☒ No

11. FATHER/PARENT 2 NAME PRIOR TO FIRST MARRIAGE	12. MOTHER/PARENT 1 NAME PRIOR TO FIRST MARRIAGE
CAROL JAMES AYMOND SR.	ORDEAN GASPARD

13. PLACE OF DEATH (CHECK ONLY ONE)

IF DEATH OCCURRED IN A HOSPITAL:	IF DEATH OCCURRED SOMEWHERE OTHER THAN A HOSPITAL:
☐ Inpatient ☐ ER/Outpatient ☐ DOA	☒ Hospice Facility ☐ Nursing Home ☐ Decedent's Home ☐ Other (Specify)

14. COUNTY OF DEATH	15. CITY/TOWN, ZIP (IF OUTSIDE CITY LIMITS, GIVE PRECINCT NO.)	16. FACILITY NAME (If not institution, give street address)
HARRIS	HOUSTON, 77045	HARBOR HOSPICE OF SOUTHEAST HOUSTON INPATIENT

17. INFORMANT'S NAME & RELATIONSHIP TO DECEASED	18. MAILING ADDRESS OF INFORMANT (Street and Number, City, State, Zip Code)
MARTHA A BORDELON - SISTER	1661 HWY 1184, COTTONPORT, LA 71327

19. METHOD OF DISPOSITION	20. SIGNATURE AND LICENSE NUMBER OF FUNERAL DIRECTOR OR PERSON ACTING AS SUCH	21. ☒ Unknown
☐ Burial ☐ Cremation ☐ Donation ☐ Entombment ☒ Removal from state ☐ Mausoleum ☐ Other (Specify)	MICHELLE NOWAK, BY ELECTRONIC SIGNATURE - 114314	Section ___ Block ___ Lot ___ Space ___

22. PLACE OF DISPOSITION (Name of cemetery, crematory, other place)	23. LOCATION (City/Town, and State)
AYMOND FAMILY CEMETERY	COTTONPORT, LA

24. NAME OF FUNERAL FACILITY	25. COMPLETE ADDRESS OF FUNERAL FACILITY (Street and Number, City, State, Zip Code)
LONESTAR MORTUARY AND CREMATIONS	4400 TOWN PLAZA DR STE 109, HOUSTON, TX 77045

26. CERTIFIER (Check only one)
☒ Certifying physician-To the best of my knowledge, death occurred due to the cause(s) and manner stated.
☐ Medical Examiner/Justice of the Peace - On the basis of examination, and/or investigation, in my opinion, death occurred at the time,date and place, and due to the cause(s) and manner stated.

27. SIGNATURE OF CERTIFIER	28. DATE CERTIFIED (mm-dd-yyyy)	29. LICENSE NUMBER	30. TIME OF DEATH (Actual or presumed)
SHERRY LEMLEY, BY ELECTRONIC SIGNATURE	MARCH 5, 2021	L8795	11:05 AM

31. PRINTED NAME, ADDRESS OF CERTIFIER (Street and Number, City,State,Zip Code)	32. TITLE OF CERTIFIER
SHERRY LEMLEY 11990 KIRBY, HOUSTON, TX 77045	MD

33. PART 1. ENTER THE CHAIN OF EVENTS - DISEASES, INJURIES, OR COMPLICATIONS - THAT DIRECTLY CAUSED THE DEATH. DO NOT ENTER TERMINAL EVENTS SUCH AS CARDIAC ARREST, RESPIRATORY ARREST, OR VENTRICULAR FIBRILLATION WITHOUT SHOWING THE ETIOLOGY. DO NOT ABBREVIATE. ENTER ONLY ONE CAUSE ON EACH.

		Approximate interval Onset to death
IMMEDIATE CAUSE (Final disease or condition resulting in death) →	a. CHRONIC RESPIRATORY FAILURE	YEARS
	Due to (or as a consequence of):	
Sequentially list conditions, if any, leading to the cause listed on line a. Enter the UNDERLYING CAUSE (disease or injury that initiated, the events resulting in death) LAST	b. IDIOPATHIC PULMONARY FIBROSIS	YEARS
	Due to (or as a consequence of):	
	c.	
	Due to (or as a consequence of):	
	d.	

PART 2. ENTER OTHER SIGNIFICANT CONDITIONS CONTRIBUTING TO DEATH BUT NOT RESULTING IN THE UNDERLYING CAUSE GIVEN IN PART I.	34. WAS AN AUTOPSY PERFORMED? ☐ Yes ☒ No
CORONARY ARTERY DISEASE, DIABETES MELLITUS	35. WERE AUTOPSY FINDINGS AVAILABLE TO COMPLETE THE CAUSE OF DEATH? ☐ Yes ☐ No

36. MANNER OF DEATH	37. DID TOBACCO USE CONTRIBUTE TO DEATH?	38. IF FEMALE:	39. IF TRANSPORTATION INJURY, SPECIFY:
☒ Natural ☐ Accident ☐ Suicide ☐ Homicide ☐ Pending Investigation ☐ Could not be determined	☐ Yes ☒ No ☐ Previously ☐ Probably ☐ Unknown	☐ Not pregnant within past year ☐ Pregnant at time of death ☐ Not pregnant, but pregnant within 42 days of death ☐ Not pregnant, but pregnant 43 days to one year before death ☐ Unknown if pregnant within the past year	☐ Driver/Operator ☐ Passenger ☐ Pedestrian ☐ Other (Specify)

40a. DATE OF INJURY (mm-dd-yyyy)	40b. TIME OF INJURY	40c. INJURY AT WORK? ☐ Yes ☐ No	40d. PLACE OF INJURY (e.g. Decedent's home, construction site, restaurant, wooded area)

40e. LOCATION (Street and Number, City,State,Zip Code)	40f. COUNTY OF INJURY

41. DESCRIBE HOW INJURY OCCURRED

MIC

42a. REGISTRAR FILE NO.	42b. DATE RECEIVED BY LOCAL REGISTRAR	42c. REGISTRAR
02005754	MARCH 12, 2021	

EDR NUMBER 000144449T6389

This is a true and correct copy of the record as registered in the State of Texas. Issued under the authority of Section 191.051, Health and Safety Code.

ISSUED   Mar 22 2021

TARA DAS
STATE REGISTRAR

THE STATE OF TEXAS

DEPARTMENT OF STATE HEALTH SERVICES VITAL STATISTICS

VS-112 REV 1/2006

QA18760964

Vernon (Pro) Ducote's Eulogy for Carol J Aymond, Jr.

Carol James Aymond, Jr., born October 23, 1946. Known to his friends as Pierre. You might ask how he got this moniker. The thing about young elementary school boys is that they observe things about their friends, and then give them a nickname. His came from Rock, Peter, and as the French would say Pierre! Needless to say, he was hardheaded! To those of us who know and love him this is not in dispute. We were born in year one of the boomer age. We were also very fortunate to grow up in the age we were born to. We had parents that survived the great depression and fought a world war. They were tough. Fathers taught us about hard work and Mothers taught us how to live in a civilized society. I think we are probably the last generation who were "free range" children. I also think we had more opportunity than any generation since. We all see people from our own perspective. A person shows many faces. One face for friends, one face for children, one face for business. I will tell you the face I saw as a friend of this remarkable man. First he was a colorful character. Smart and gifted with a work ethic that required long days and hard work. That work ethic produced a great career, three wonderful children, and wealth. We became friends in the third grade. The wonder of it was that we became friends at all. For several days this little twerp would run up to me during recess and punch me in the stomach, laugh, and run off. After a couple of days of this, I devised a plan to stop his behavior, without beating the snot out of him. I wore a large cowboy belt buckle to school. After I got out of my mother's sight, I pulled my shirt out of my pants to disguise the buckle. On cue during recess, he ran up to me and swung hard. The look on his face was truly priceless and that ended his punches. We became friends. We played midget football and junior varsity, but in our freshman year he quit. Guess he got tired of the two of us being assigned two laps around the football field every day after practice. That was the only time I ever saw him quit anything he wanted to do. His iron will and hard head usually carried him through.

When he finished high school, he was off to LSU. He earned an undergraduate degree and decided to go to law school. Uncle Sam had other ideas about his future. He was drafted by the Army for two years to fight the war in Vietnam. Offered an officer commission, he said no. While in recruit training he was selected for the Army's Instant Non-commissioned Officer Program. After boot camp he went to Non-commissioned Officer's school, completed the course, and was promoted to Sergeant. It took me four years to make Sergeant! He went off to Vietnam as a Squad Leader. He and I happened to be there at the same time. I was on my second tour there and unfortunately; we could not get together. For his service in Vietnam, he was awarded the Bronze Star and left the Army as a Staff Sergeant.

Since high school we always remained in touch no matter where in the world I was. No matter how busy he was he always had time to take my phone call, laugh and share stories. We visited when we could, always found adventure, and thoroughly enjoyed each other's company. Walter Winchell said of friendship, "A real friend is one who walks in when the rest of the world walks out." When I needed a friend or he needed a friend, we were always there for each other. True friendships are forged by adversity. Adversity tests the bonds of friends, not the good times.

Now for the Pierre quirks. Yes, he had a few! He loved to travel and loved the mountains. He would occasionally just get in his car and drive to a mountain somewhere. He would not fly due to his experiences in the First Air Calvary Division in Vietnam. I don't remember a time going to his house that FOX News was not on the television. He loved listening to the oldies we grew up on, especially sitting in front of a fireplace. He rarely had more than two drinks and had the nasty habit of putting Coke in his whiskey. I could never cure him of that. He would barbecue with plastic salad tongs. Hunted pheasants with my wife Dee Ann and me on several occasions with his 16 gauge. He really loved that shotgun. He never liked shooting my shotgun; he said they kicked too much. Maybe that had something to do with me always loading buckshot in them before I handed the shotgun to him to shoot. He was the only person I've ever canoed with that wore cowboy boots; and he discovered cowboy boots were not the best thing to wear when getting off a ski lift on top of a mountain in Colorado.

He loved wood and paneled his house with oak and cypress. He showed up at my house on several occasions with a unique pieces of lumber that he wanted me to build furniture with. We smoked Cuban cigars that mysteriously appeared in my luggage on one of my exploits out of the country. He screamed like a baby at a terrifying 100 miles per hour on the back of my motorcycle. He could tell you the genealogy of ever cow he owned back three or more generations.

Shopping locally with Pierre was a chore. He would be stopped many times by folks asking questions and wanting legal advice. He always stopped what he was doing, treated them with kindness and compassion, doing his best to address their problems.

Pierre was devoted to the church and his Catholic faith. He was generous with his time, thrifty with his money, and always welcoming. Lastly, he always had a bottle of Jack Daniels ready for me when I visited. Now, that's a true friend! His daughter Chantel and I were there for his lung transplant. It took courage to go through what he endured. We all knew it would be a long road to recovery and not an easy road to travel. Pierre faced his fate with dignity and a belief in God. A special thanks goes to his sisters Martha and Darla. Without their support and care he would not have lasted as long as he did. Martha, you did Yeoman's work taking care of his affairs and I do hope you will be rewarded in heaven.

If I had to select a song to describe Pierre's life, that song would be "My Way". He truly did things his way. Seldom in life does a person get to do so. Pierre, you were my friend, my brother, and I will miss you . I am very lucky to have known you and called you "my friend". Another bulb has gone out on my tree of life, but, that light will be everlasting in me.

Chapter 10:   Arthur David and Susan Laborde Aymond

David was born on February 5, 1957 at the Knoll Clinic in Bunkie, LA.   He was the fifth of five children of Carol and Ordean Aymond. David was reared with his four siblings in Dora Bend, between Cottonport and Evergreen on Highway 1184.

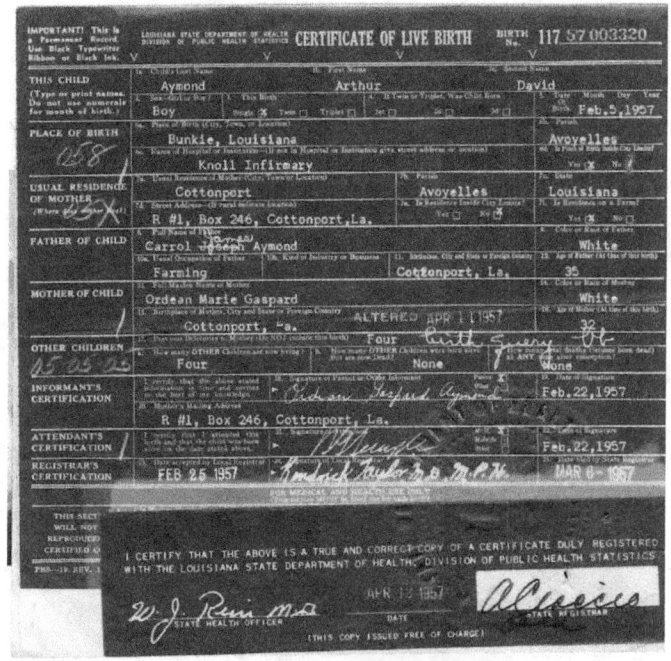

Husband: Arthur David Aymond
DOB: February 5, 1957, Bunkie, LA
Married: May 27, 1978
Died:
Buried:
Where:

Wife: Susan Gayle Laborde
DOB: 01/14/58, Cottonport, LA
Father: Wilford Laborde
Mother: Jacquline "Jackie" Michott

Children:

Name	DOB - DOD	Married	Comments (education, etc.)
Leslie	DOB: 06-11-80 M: 6/21-2003	Jason Hatchett (Divorced)	Received her B.A. in Accounting from L.S.U. in Baton Rouge in 2003 and became a CPA. They have two children: Twins, Kalli Nicole and Brody Todd, born October 15, 2007.
Jennifer	DOB: 05-07-82 M: 11/4/2006 M: 1/9/2010	Curt Bone (Divorced) Jimmy Picone	Received her R.N. Degree from L.S.U. and then Nurse Practioner Degree. She and Jimmy have two children, Abbigail and Josua.
Heather	DOB: 01-12-84		Received her R.N. Degree from L.S.U. and then Nurse Practioner Degree. She has a daughter, Ellie.
Joshua	DOB: 01-21-88		Received a B.S. in Biological Sciences from L.S.U. He later earned a Medical Degree at L.S.U. New Orleans. He has a daughter, Audrey.
Tyler	DOB: 06-30-92		Attended and received a Business Degree from L.S.U.

Like his brothers and sisters, David attended Cottonport Elementary School. He later attended and graduated in 1974 from Central Louisiana Academy in Bunkie. After high school graduation, he attended LSU in Alexandria. He later transferred to Louisiana State University in Baton Rouge where he earned a B.S. in Civil Engineering in 1979.

Susan graduated from Cottonport High School and then received her R.N. Degree from Louisiana State University at Alexandria in 1978. On May 27, 1978, David and Susan were married at St. Mary's Assumption Church in Cottonport.

David with his parents,
 Carol and
Ordean Gaspard Aymond

David with his sister, Martha.

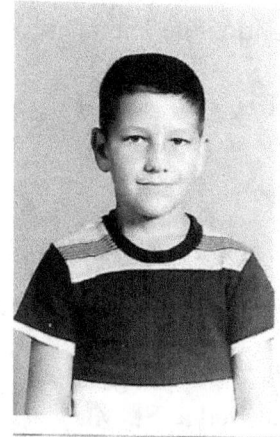

161

The Wedding Party:

L to R: Darla, Martha, Chris Bordelon, Ordean Aymond, Susan Laborde Aymond, David Aymond, Carol Aymond, Sr., Donna Aymond, Carol Aymond, Jr. Front Row: Emma Aymond (David's paternal grandmother), Jamie Aymond, Kristin Bordelon, Mary Louise Gaspard (David's maternal grandmother)

Graduation from Central Louisiana Academy in Bunkie, LA

1974 GRADUATES

Class Flower: Mums (Yellow & White)
Class Motto: Today we Follow, Tomorrow we Lead

Ramona Antie	Robert Blake Newton
Arthur David Aymond	Laurie Marie Nick
Nancy Ann Baudin	David Gerald Ormsby
Maria Isobelle Chautin	Duane Floyd Ortego
Rose Marie Chautin	Debra Lane Pettit
Terry Scott Clopton	John Edward Pickett
Jacquelyn Anne Doucet	Susan Gremillion Pickett
Nolan Louis Ducote	Thomas Ardie Pickett
Daphni Dawn Ellerbee	Susan Ann Reynaud
Karen Joan Francois	Jo Ann Rowley
Camille Anne Johnson	Pamela Marie Sabatini
Michael Lawrence Keller	Pamela Bernadette Smith
Mary Rose Lipoma	Chester Sylvester III
Belinda Kaye Middlebrooks	Cynthia Rose Townsend
Marshall Stanley Mouliere, Jr.	Janet Ruth Townsend
Carl Anthony Newton	John H. Voorhies, Jr.

Jack C. Williams, Jr.

Master of Ceremonies
Michael Keller
President C. L. A. Student Council

PROGRAM

Processional	Graduates
	Music, Mr. Merkel Dupuy
Invocation	Rev. Vernon Bordelon
Pledge of Allegiance	Michael Keller
	Senior Class President
Salutatorian	Mary Rose Lipoma
Sunshine on my Shoulder	Class Song
Valedictorian	Marshall Mouliere
Those were the Days	Class Song
American Legion Awards	Mr. Chester Hebert
Commencement Address	Dr. Donald Hines
Morning Has Broken	Class Song
Awarding Diplomas	Mr. William Pearce
	Mr. Edwin J. Bozek
Long and Winding Road	Class Song
Benediction	Rev. Vernon Bordelon
Recessional	Mr. Merkel Dupuy

DAVID A. AYMOND

BROADHURST, BROOK,
MANGHAM, HARDY & REED
ATTORNEYS AND COUNSELORS AT LAW
THE FIRST NATIONAL BANK TOWERS, SUITE 1400

P. O. DRAWER 2879
LAFAYETTE, LA. 70502
(318) 233-6200

After working in the engineering field with a firm in Baton Rouge for a year, David decided to pursue a degree in law from L.S.U. In 1983, he received his Juris Doctorate from L.S.U. David worked for two years as an attorney in Lafayette at Broadhust/Brooks. In 1986, he and his family moved to Gainesville, Florida where he attend the University of Florida and earned a Master of Law and Tax. Between 1986-1992 he practiced law in Mandeville, LA. During this time, he began his business in subdivision construction. By 1996 he devoted all his time to his business Aymond Construction.

163

Louisiana State University Law School 1983

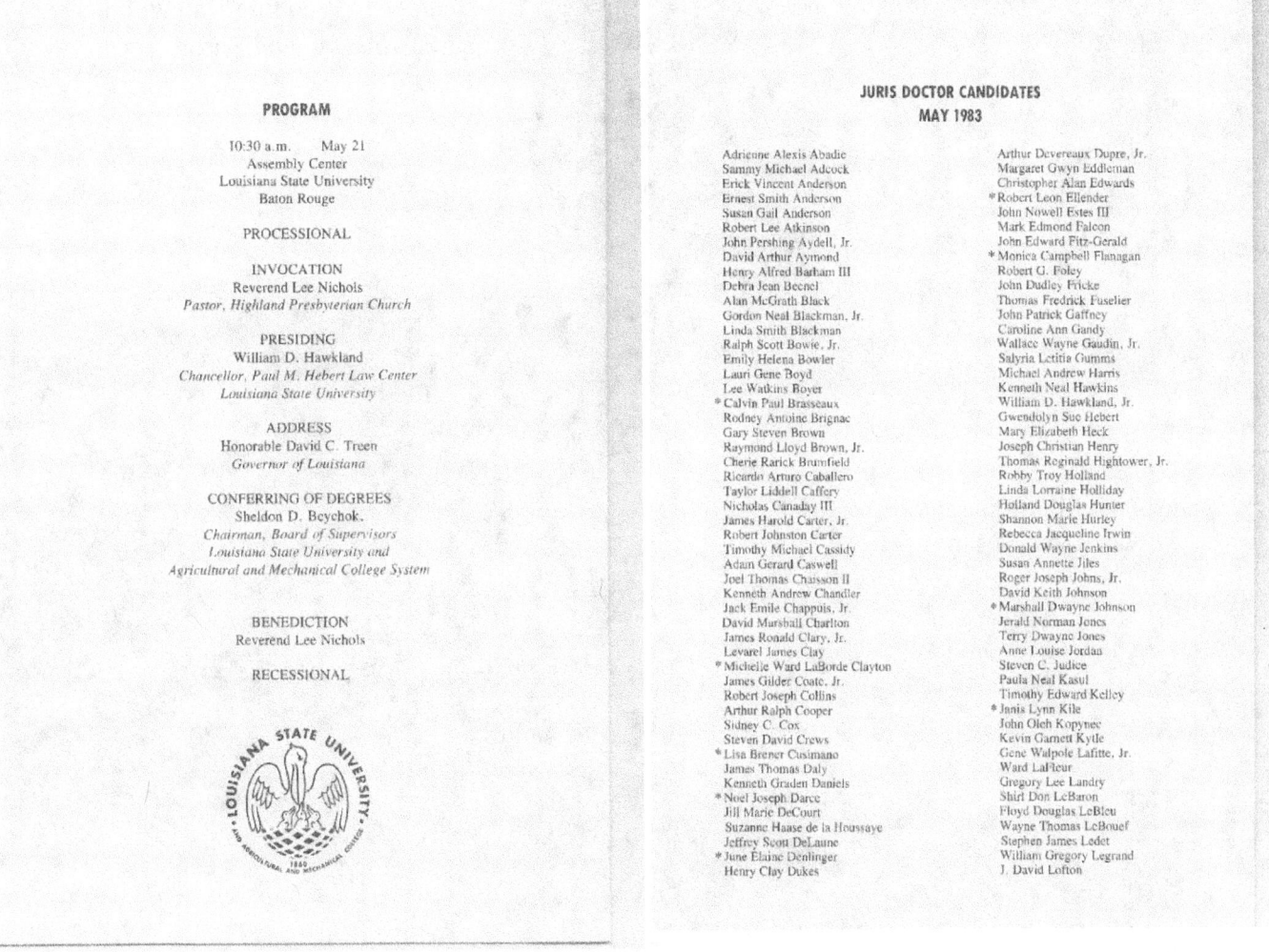

PROGRAM

10:30 a.m.   May 21
Assembly Center
Louisiana State University
Baton Rouge

PROCESSIONAL

INVOCATION
Reverend Lee Nichols
Pastor, Highland Presbyterian Church

PRESIDING
William D. Hawkland
Chancellor, Paul M. Hebert Law Center
Louisiana State University

ADDRESS
Honorable David C. Treen
Governor of Louisiana

CONFERRING OF DEGREES
Sheldon D. Beychok
Chairman, Board of Supervisors
Louisiana State University and
Agricultural and Mechanical College System

BENEDICTION
Reverend Lee Nichols

RECESSIONAL

JURIS DOCTOR CANDIDATES
MAY 1983

Adrienne Alexis Abadie
Sammy Michael Adcock
Erick Vincent Anderson
Ernest Smith Anderson
Susan Gail Anderson
Robert Lee Atkinson
John Pershing Aydell, Jr.
David Arthur Aymond
Henry Alfred Barham III
Debra Jean Becnel
Alan McGrath Black
Gordon Neal Blackman, Jr.
Linda Smith Blackman
Ralph Scott Bowie, Jr.
Emily Helena Bowler
Lauri Gene Boyd
Lee Watkins Boyer
* Calvin Paul Brasseaux
Rodney Antoine Brignac
Gary Steven Brown
Raymond Lloyd Brown, Jr.
Cherie Rarick Brumfield
Ricardo Arturo Caballero
Taylor Liddell Caffery
Nicholas Canaday III
James Harold Carter, Jr.
Robert Johnston Carter
Timothy Michael Cassidy
Adam Gerard Caswell
Joel Thomas Chaisson II
Kenneth Andrew Chandler
Jack Emile Chappuis, Jr.
David Marshall Charlton
James Ronald Clary, Jr.
Levarel James Clay
* Michelle Ward LaBorde Clayton
James Gilder Coate, Jr.
Robert Joseph Collins
Arthur Ralph Cooper
Sidney C. Cox
Steven David Crews
* Lisa Brener Cusimano
James Thomas Daly
Kenneth Graden Daniels
* Noel Joseph Darce
Jill Marie DeCourt
Suzanne Haase de la Houssaye
Jeffrey Scott DeLaune
* June Elaine Denlinger
Henry Clay Dukes

Arthur Devereaux Dupre, Jr.
Margaret Gwyn Eddleman
Christopher Alan Edwards
* Robert Leon Ellender
John Nowell Estes III
Mark Edmond Falcon
John Edward Fitz-Gerald
* Monica Campbell Flanagan
Robert G. Foley
John Dudley Fricke
Thomas Fredrick Fuselier
John Patrick Gaffney
Caroline Ann Gandy
Wallace Wayne Gaudin, Jr.
Salyria Letitia Gumms
Michael Andrew Harris
Kenneth Neal Hawkins
William D. Hawkland, Jr.
Gwendolyn Sue Hebert
Mary Elizabeth Heck
Joseph Christian Henry
Thomas Reginald Hightower, Jr.
Robby Troy Holland
Linda Lorraine Holliday
Holland Douglas Hunter
Shannon Marie Hurley
Rebecca Jacqueline Irwin
Donald Wayne Jenkins
Susan Annette Jiles
Roger Joseph Johns, Jr.
David Keith Johnson
* Marshall Dwayne Johnson
Jerald Norman Jones
Terry Dwayne Jones
Anne Louise Jordan
Steven C. Judice
Paula Neal Kasul
Timothy Edward Kelley
* Janis Lynn Kile
John Oleh Kopynec
Kevin Garnett Kytle
Gene Walpole Lafitte, Jr.
Ward LaFleur
Gregory Lee Landry
Shirl Don LeBaron
Floyd Douglas LeBleu
Wayne Thomas LeBouef
Stephen James Ledet
William Gregory Legrand
J. David Lofton

.   David and Susan have five children; Leslie, Jennifer, Heather, Joshua, and Tyler. Two of his girls, Jennifer and Heather have a master's degrees in nursing and work as Family Nurse Practitioners. Jennifer has two children, Abigail and Joshua Picone. Heather has two children. She and her partner of many years, Roger Watson, have two children Ellie and Emily Watson. Leslie is a CPA and is married to Jason Hatchett. They have two children; Brody and Kalli.

Jennifer's Wedding Day with her parents, David and Susan

Joshua with his parents, David and Susan

Leslie and Jason's Wedding Day

David and Susan's Family:

Joshua, Heather, Jimmy and Jenny Aymond Picone,

Tyler and Leslie Aymond Hatchett

Chapter 11: The Next Aymond Generation

Burton Aymond, Jr. was born on November 29, 1959 in New Orleans, La   He attended and graduated from Bonnabel High School in 1977. He also attended Rets Electronic Training Institute.

In 1977, Burton married Barbara Perez from New Orleans. They have two children, Jeffery and Jennifer.

At the age of 15, he worked as a Black & Decker repairman, later, a Caterpillar forklift installer. He now owns and operates three daycare/school businesses.

His hobbies include: metal fabrication and astronomy. He designed and built a world class astronomical observatory at his home in New Orleans.

Kirk Aymond was born in New Orleans on November 17, 1965. He was the second son of Burton Aymond and Helena Dauzat. He graduated from East Jefferson High School in 1983.   He earned a degree in Electrical Engineering from the University of New Orleans and a degree in Environmental Management from Louisiana State University. He has been employed at Pellerin Milnor Corporation in Kenner, LA since 1984. He is presently employed as the Plant Superintendent. He also taught astrophysics at the University of New Orleans in 2005-2010. Kirk's hobbies include hiking, astronomy, mechanical design and fabrication. He also holds a private pilot's license since 1986.

Carol James (Jamie) Aymond, III was born on February 14, 1970. He was the first of two children of Carol Aymond, Jr. and Donna Ducote Aymond with his sister Chantel. He graduated from Bunkie High School and attended LSU in Baton Rouge. He married Deborah Bruner on February 4, 1994 at St. Anne's Catholic Church in Beaumont, TX. He and Deborah had two children, Weston James (12/16/99) and Julia Rose (7/22/05). He and his children resided in LaGrange, TX. Jamie presently works for Union Pacific Railroad.

Joshua Aymond was born on January 21, 1988. He was the fourth of five children of David and Susan Laborde Aymond. Joshua grew up in Mandeville with his four siblings; Leslie, Jennifer, Heather, and Tyler. Joshua graduated from Mandeville High School and then went on to Louisiana State University where he earned a degree in Biological Sciences in 2010. He graduated from LSU Health Science Center School of Medicine at New Orleans. He is now a certified Internal Medicine Physician. He is currently completing a Fellowship in Cardiology with Ochsner Hospital in New Orleans. Joshua married Morgan Silvio on December 8, 2018.

Tyler Aymond was born on June 30, 1992. He was the last of five children of David and Susan Aymond. Tyler grew up in Mandeville, LA. He played baseball at Mandeville High. He graduated from Mandeville High School in 2011 and went on to earn a Business Degree from Louisiana State University in Baton Rouge. He is presently an Associate Partner at New York Life Insurance Company, New Orleans, LA.

Weston James Aymond is one of two children of Carol (Jamie) Aymond, III and Deborah Bruner Aymond. He was born on December 16, 1999. He resides with his father and sister, Julia Rose, in LaGrange, Texas. He is presently attending Texas A & M University in College Station, Texas.

Other Family Members

Darla Aymond with her children; Amanda Normand, Scotty Normand and Trent Murchison

Carol Aymond, Sr. with great grandkids; Allison Normand, Christopher Normand, Bethany Scallan, Grace Bordelon, and Brian Johnson (grandchildren of Martha Aymond and Chris Bordelon)

Darla Aymond and Martha Aymond Bordelon in Europe, 2012

Randy Guillory Aymond, son of Terrell
Guillory and Crystal Aymond

This picture was taken one Christmas at Carol Aymond, Jr.'s home near Evergreen, LA.

Front Row: Joshua Aymond, Martha Aymond Bordelon, Carol Aymond, Sr., Ordean Gaspard Aymond, Leslie Aymond, Tyler Aymond

Middle Row: David Aymond, Darla Aymond, Amanda Normand

Back Row: Kirk Aymond, Pauline Aymond, Burton Aymond, Crystal Aymond, Susan Laborde Aymond, Christopher Bordelon, Vickie Aymond, Helena Dauzat Aymond, Brandon (Vickie's son), and Heather Aymond

170

To My Aymond Family:

It is my hope that someone in my family will continue to add information to our family tree. As expressed in the following poem by Willis G. Corbitt, a family tree is never finished.

The Family Tree

I think that I shall never see

The finish of a family tree,

As it forever seems to grow

Way back in Ancient History times,

In foreign lands and distant climes

From them grew trunk and branching limb

That dated back to times so dim,

One seldom knows exactly when

The parents met and married then,

Nor when the twigs began to grow

With off named children, row on row,

Though a verse like this is made by me

And the end's in sight, as you can see,

T'is not the same with family trees

That grow through centuries.

Contact me at marth-ab@hotmail.com for any corrections or additions. I hope you enjoy reading about your ancestor; I enjoyed putting it together.

Martha Aymond Bordelon